MASTERING

SPREADSH

CW00594817

MACMILLAN MASTER SERIES

Astronomy
Australian History
Background to Business
Banking
Basic English Law
Basic Management
Biology
British Politics
Business Communication
Business Law
Business Microcomputing
Catering Science
Catering Theory
Chemistry
COBOL Programming
Commerce
Computer Programming
Computers
Data Processing
Economic and Social History
Economics
Electrical Engineering
Electronics
English Grammar
English Language
English Literature
Financial Accounting
French
French 2

German
German 2
Hairdressing
Italian
Japanese
Keyboarding
Marketing
Mathematics
Modern British History
Modern European History
Modern World History
Nutrition
Office Practice
Pascal Programming
Physics
Practical Writing
Principles of Accounts
Restaurant Science
Social Welfare
Sociology
Spanish
Spanish 2
Spreadsheets
Statistics
Statistics with your Microcomputer
Study Skills
Typewriting Skills
Word Processing

MASTERING
SPREADSHEETS

PETER GOSLING

MACMILLAN

First published 1989

Published by
MACMILLAN EDUCATION LTD
Houndmills, Basingstoke, Hampshire RG21 2XS
and London
Companies and representatives
throughout the world

Typeset by TecSet Ltd, Wallington, Surrey

Printed in the People's Republic of China

British Library Cataloguing in Publication Data
Gosling, P. E. (Peter Edward)
Mastering spreadsheets. – (Macmillan
master series).
1. Microcomputer systems. Spreadsheet
packages
I. Title
005.36′9
ISBN 0–333–47228–4
ISBN 0–333–47229–2 Pbk
ISBN 0–333–47230–6 Pbk export

CONTENTS

CONTENTS

PREFACE

Now that more and more PCs (Personal Computers) are finding their way onto the desks of more and more (and more senior) managers in industry the time has come for a book to be written not about particular pieces of software but about the ideas behind the use of a generic type of program. Already in the Macmillan Master Series we have two books in this vein. Mastering Computer Programming tells the aspiring programmer about the various sorts of computer languages available and why they are suited for certain types of tasks and Mastering Word Processing describes the jobs that a word processing program can do for us. The programs we buy to run on our PCs are nothing more or less than solutions looking for problems to solve and we are in no position to make a judgement on whether or not we are likely to need such a program if we are unaware of the power available to us through these programs.

Mastering Spreadsheets will give you a general, but detailed, description of what spreadsheet programs can do and then the last chapter describes the features of a number of the best selling spreadsheets on the market. No attempt is made to say if one is better than any other. It is well known that when somebody purchases a piece of computer software for their PC they only use some 20% to 25% of the full potential of the program. This book will allow you to make the correct decision when you come to select a spreadsheet program. There are too many suppliers of software who will try and sell you a program because it is expensive, and hence their profit is greater, not because it does the job you require of it easily and cheaply. Do not be put off by a program just because it is cheap. It may do exactly what you want without the need to plot complex three-dimensional graphs or perform matrix inversion.

My thanks are due to Migent (UK), Grafox Ltd, MicroSoft Inc, Persona (UK), Borland International and Lotus Development Corp for supplying copies of their latest software without which this book could not have been completed.

TRADEMARKS

Ability Plus is a trademark of Migent International Corporation
Boeing Calc is a trademark of Boeing Computer Services
dBASE II and dBASE III are trademarks of Ashton-Tate
Excel is a trademark of MicroSoft Corporation
Framework is a trademark of Ashton-Tate
HAL is a trademark of Lotus Development Corporation
IBM is a trademark of IBM Corporation
Logistix is a trademark of Grafox Ltd
Lotus 1-2-3 is a trademark of Lotus Development Corporation
MS-DOS is a trademark of MicroSoft Corporation
Multiplan is a trademark of MicroSoft Corporation
PC-DOS is a trademark of IBM Corporation
Perfect Calc II is a trademark of Perfect Software
Quattro is a trademark of Borland International
Sideways is a trademark of Funck Software
SuperCalc is a trademark of Computer Associates
Symphony is a trademark of Lotus Development Corporation

INTRODUCTION

1.1 WHAT THIS BOOK IS ABOUT

This book is an introduction to using spreadsheets, or worksheets as they are sometimes called, and the capabilities of a number of the popular spreadsheet programs. It is not intended to replace the comprehensive manuals supplied with each spreadsheet program. Unfortunately some of these manuals can be rather frightening for the newcomer and so this book provides a gentle lead-in to the full story provided by the manufacturers. Manuals are very useful if you know what you are looking for and if you want to know, for example, how to deal with copying, replicating, windowing and recalculation - always assuming you realise what these things are in the first place. This book provides an overview of the most common spreadsheet facilities and how they can help to improve and enhance the work that you process. All spreadsheet programs will allow you to perform a series of basic numerical manipulation operations, but some will offer a number of extremely sophisticated additional functions, some of which you may need desperately and some of which you may not find of value in your particular business.

You will probably make the most dreadful mistakes in the early stages of using one of these programs and the whole thing will appear to be just a jumble of unrelated figures until suddenly the end of the tunnel appears and you will wonder what all the fuss was about. What you will also discover is that you will rarely use all the facilities offered by the spreadsheet you have, but at least when you do have to use one of the more obscure features you will have the confidence to try it out.

Many computer manufacturers are coming to realise that there is a great need for more "user friendliness" and so more helpful systems are being produced with liberal help facilities. These make life a great deal easier for the new user. Practice, as usual, makes perfect, and remember always to read what is on the screen!

1.2 INTRODUCING THE PERSONAL COMPUTER

The now very popular personal computer (PC) is a system with a very wide range of uses of which one is that it enables you to create and use powerful spreadsheet programs. It derives its versatility from the fact that it can accept information from a keyboard, very similar to that on a conventional typewriter, store it, display it on a video screen, manipulate it according to a program of instructions and then deliver it out on to a printing device. How this is actually accomplished luckily does not concern the average user at all. But like all systems one has to learn how it needs to be treated, what liberties can be taken with it, and just what its limitations are.

However complex such a system is made out to be it can never do anything that a human being cannot do. Despite assertions to the contrary it is extremely difficult to destroy all the information you have stored away. Not only that, but computers do not make mistakes; people make mistakes. Computers do as they are told quite blindly. So if you come across a situation where someone says, "but it has just cleared everything off the screen!" then they must have done something to make that happen. Computers both large and small never do anything of their own volition.

The main parts of the modern PC are the keyboard, which is your way into the machine, the screen and the printer, which are its channels of communication with the outside world, the electronics that perform the manipulation of data and some form of disk storage.

A typical PC keyboard is shown in Figure 1.1. You should notice that it is just like a normal typewriter keyboard but with a number of additions. Three of the most important keys are the one marked **RETURN**, or **Enter**, the one marked **Ctrl** and the one marked **Esc**. Some word processors use the key marked **Alt** as well. The first of these is the key that is usually used tell the computer that you have finished your instruction. In a spreadsheet we use the four arrow keys to move the cursor - that's the flashing line or block on the screen indicating one cell on the sheet. These arrow keys are found on the right of the typewriter keys on the keyboard in what is called a "numeric pad". The 8, 2, 6 and 4 keys have arrows on them that enable you to move the cursor about the screen. The Escape (Esc) key is your "panic button". If anything goes wrong while you are using your computer then if you press this key you can usually stop whatever is happening. To the left of the keyboard, or across the top in some cases, are a series of "function" keys, lettered F1 to F10. These are keys used by many spreadsheets to carry out operations that would otherwise require more than one keystroke.

Fig 1.1 *PC keyboard*

The key marked F1 is often used as a "HELP" key. Press that, or its equivalent, and you will be given help relevant to what is happening at that moment; these keys are said to be "context related". This is particularly helpful while editing a worksheet. The key marked "Home" is used by some spreadsheets to take the cursor to the top left hand corner of the sheet. In order to use it in its alternative mode, as a numeric key pad, press the "Num Lock" key.

The electronics hidden away inside what is called the "system box" or "system unit" perform two main functions. The first of these is the electronic manipulation of data and is performed by the now famous "microprocessor". Contrary to what you see in the press and on television, the microprocessor is not an electronic "brain". It actually operates like a telephone switchboard directing data to the appropriate parts of the machine. It also manages to perform simple arithmetic when required.

The second important part of the electronics is the memory, called RAM for Random Access Memory, which operates very much like our own memory in that it can retain a set of instructions on how a task is to be performed together with the data to be manipulated within that task. In other words the PC's memory has to be able to retain all the program instructions and the data being processed on the sheet.

For long-term storage the PC uses magnetic disks, either the small removable "floppy" disks or one of these disks in conjunction with a "hard" disk. A floppy disk on most PCs will store approximately 360,000 characters (360 kilobytes: 1 keystroke = 1 character = 1 byte) and the hard disk, sometimes called a "Winchester" disk, can store anything from 10 million characters (10 Megabytes) upwards. The reason for the use of the term "floppy" and "hard" is that the former type are made of thin plastic material which is then covered with a magnetic coating and the latter type consist of a set of rigid aluminium disks coated with a magnetic substance. Floppy disks come in a sealed square pack with a slot along a radius that allows the magnetic read and write head to fly over the surface of the disk. Under no circumstances should you touch the exposed surface of the disk. Dust and grease are death to the data on the disk. Never attempt to clean them by rubbing with a duster! Always use one of the cleaning devices recommended by your dealer.

Always insert a disk label side upward into the disk drive and press it gently home; then lock it into position with the locking button or lever. This is shown in Figure 1.2. You should notice that on the left-hand side of the disk package there is a small square cut out. This can be covered with one of the small sticky tabs supplied with all new boxes of disks. When the cut out is covered the computer cannot write data to the disk and can only read data from it. The disk is then said to be "write-protected". If the cut out is not covered then the disk can be written to and read from and the write-protection is removed.

Hard disks come in a sealed box and normally cannot be removed from the machine. All types of disks work in a similar way to a domestic tape recorder, in fact these were what were used for storage on the first generation of microcomputers.

Fig 1.2 *Inserting a disk*

The programs you buy for your PC are always supplied on floppy disks. You must always make a copy of these programs on to other floppy disks, or to a hard disk, before using them. The original disks can then be stored away for safety and the program is run from the copies. You need to transfer these programs from disk into the memory of your PC before they can be run. This is called "loading the program". The work sheets you create with your spreadsheet program are also stored on disk so that they can be recalled when required. What you have to appreciate before you use a spreadsheet in practice is that there is a difference between a "program" and the "data" it uses. The program is a static set of rules and instructions that your PC will carry out in order to allow you to create and edit sets of data. The data consists of the numbers and the formulas you enter at the keyboard.

Spreadsheet data is entered initially by you at the keyboard and displayed on the screen as you proceed with your typing. Once a worksheet is on the screen, which means that you are seeing a copy of what is stored in the RAM, you can manipulate it as you wish. You can change parts of the sheet, move parts of it about and delete parts of it. All this affects the data that is held in the memory. When you have completed your editing of a sheet you can save it away on to a magnetic disk, clear the sheet out of the memory and start off on the editing or preparation of another. This might give you an inkling of one of the great advantages of using a spreadsheet. It is that many offices have the requirement constantly to recalculate the same set of formulas using different figures each time, for a cash flow forecast for example. Or you might wish to produce an up-to-date sales forecast based on the latest sales figures. It may even be that you want to display data in a graphical form for greater impact. Most modern spreadsheet programs will do this for you.

1.3 PRINTERS AND PLOTTERS

The final product from any spreadsheet must be a set of figures. There are now a variety of printing devices that can be used to produce the finished output. Until quite recently there were only two kinds of printer available. One was the "dot matrix" type where a bundle of wires are fired on to the paper through a ribbon. The pattern of wires produces the character to be printed made up of a series of dots. With early printers of this type the print quality was reasonable but not considered to be acceptable for official documents and important letters. The other was the "daisy wheel" type where the printer is more like an electronic typewriter. The characters are placed around a series of stalks fixed to a central hub and moved to the correct position above the paper before being pressed down on to a ribbon by a small hammer. The daisy wheel is removable and this enables a wide range of character styles to be used.

Recently dot matrix printers have improved rapidly in quality and many of them can now print in at least two modes: draft mode where the speed is around 200 characters a second and the print quality is only reasonable, and NLQ (Near Letter Quality) where the speed is much slower but the quality is as high as many daisy wheel printers. In addition, a dot matrix printer can be used to plot graphs if required. This is something a daisywheel printer cannot do.

A further refinement available now is the ink jet printer where instead of series of pins being fired a series of jets of ink are squirted on to the paper. This has the advantage of being far quieter than either a dot matrix or a daisy wheel printer. It also produces a very high quality character due to the way that ink spots spread slightly on the paper, eliminating the dots.

The latest development in printer technology is the laser printer. This is a development of the photocopier and is capable of producing the highest quality output, both as text and figures or as a graph.

Another device of use with a spreadsheet program is the plotter where graphs can be produced to a very high standard by drawing the graph on paper with a pen. With these devices the paper usually moves while the pen stays still. Some of the plotters can have several pens containing different coloured inks which can be selected by the spreadsheet software to produce graphs in full colour.

It is of paramount importance to make sure that the spreadsheet program knows exactly which printer is connected so that full use is made of the facilities it offers. There are over 250 different printers available at the present time and they are not all identical by any means. Apart from the differences in manufacturer there are various types and sub-types you may have to make allowances for.

Ignoring for the moment that there are several different ways of transferring characters on to paper there are two basic ways for your machine to communicate with a printer. These are "serial" and "parallel". The serial socket will sometimes be known as "the RS 232 port" and may be labelled as such.

If you bear in mind that the printer obtains its instructions by a series of electrical pulses sent down the wires connecting it to the computer then it is this pattern of pulses that tell it to print a letter "A", a letter "a" or a graphics character.

In simple terms, the instructions to a printer come in sets of eight and they can be sent to the printer in one of two ways appropriate to the design of the printer. A "serial" printer expects the pulses to be sent "serially" to it, which means that the eight pulses are sent one after the other along a pair or wires. A "parallel" printer expects all eight to be sent simultaneously along a set of eight parallel wires. A piece of electronics inside the printer then decodes these pulses and arranges for the correct character to be printed. In fact, each printer contains a small computer in order to handle this operation.

If you have purchased a serial printer then it must be plugged into the socket at the back of your computer marked "SERIAL" or "SERIAL PORT". A parallel printer must be plugged into the "PARALLEL" socket. A parallel port is sometimes known as a "Centronics" port.

The most popular types of printer are of the parallel type, but you should check just to make sure, because when the installation routine is running you should be ready to answer the question "Is it a parallel or serial printer?" correctly.

Most word processors can handle the various types of printer and you will usually have a list displayed from which you can tell the program the make and type of printer you have. This usually takes care of the daisy wheel/dot matrix choice.

There are a number of dot matrix printers these days that can print, and plot, in colour and so if you are going to use one of these you will need to tell the INSTALL program that you intend to use one.

Plotters are available in one of two types. One of these is the "flat bed" plotter where a sheet of paper is laid on a table over which a pen, or several pens if you are going to plot in colour, moves. A plotter of this sort is shown in Figure 1.3. The other type of plotter is one that uses conventional continuous stationery with one or more pens fixed above a roller. The

roller guides the paper underneath the pens as the graph
is drawn. A plotter of this type is shown in Figure 1.4.

Fig 1.3 *Flat bed plotter (Photograph courtesy of
Hewlett-Packard Ltd)*

Fig 1.4 *Moving paper plotter (Photograph courtesy of
Hewlett-Packard Ltd)*

1.4 LOOKING AT THE OPERATING SYSTEM

In order to get your PC ready to work you have to go through the procedure known as "booting it up". This is the name given to the operation of loading a special program called the "operating system" into its memory so that it is ready to receive and run your spreadsheet program. Before the operating system has been loaded into memory your PC is a fairly useless chunk of electronics. The operating system breathes life into your PC in the same way that Frankenstein used the forces of Nature to breathe "life" into his monster. There are certainly a large number of people who believe that the analogy is a very close one! Once the operating system has been loaded your PC is in a position to accept instructions from the keyboard and carry them out. Of course, at this stage it will only understand operating system commands. It is only when your spreadsheet program has been loaded as well that your PC will be able to "talk" Lotus 1-2-3, SuperCalc or whatever spreadsheet you are using. You should note that at all times the operating system and the spreadsheet program are both stored in memory together. This is because you "talk" to the spreadsheet via the keyboard, and it can then, itself, communicate with the operating system to tell it to carry out certain instructions. For example, in all spreadsheets there is a command to save a worksheet on disk. You type this in at the keyboard and instruct Lotus 1-2-3, for example, to save the sheet. The Lotus 1-2-3 program then issues the instruction to the operating system to perform the saving operation. When the sheet has been safely saved on to a disk the operating system tells Lotus that this has been done, and Lotus then informs you.

You know when the operating system is safely installed in the memory because the screen stops displaying a lot of apparently technical information, although you are often asked to type in the date and the time of day, and will display what is known as a "system prompt". This takes the form of a letter of the alphabet followed by a small arrow

A>

or

C>

The devices containing the disks, floppy or hard, are known a "drives" and they are referred to by letters of the alphabet. If you have a PC, or a PC compatible, with two floppy disk drives then they are known as drive A and drive B. If you have a machine with a single floppy disk drive and a hard disk then the floppy disk is known as drive A and the hard disk is known as drive C. The letter displayed on the screen is that referring to the drive currently in use, the "logged disk drive". This is the drive the operating system is looking at. If you have a machine with twin floppy drives you can remove the DOS (Disk Operating System) disk from drive A; it contains the master operating system program that has now been copied into memory. This disk should always be kept in a safe place, for without it your PC cannot be started up. Now you can replace this disk with one that contains the spreadsheet program and load that into memory as well. Then you are ready to start creating and using spreadsheets.

General instructions for the starting of spreadsheet programs will be detailed a little later.

Once your operating system program has been safely loaded into memory there are a number of things it can do for you either before or after you have used a spreadsheet. The operating system, usually called MS-DOS (MicroSoft Disk Operating System) or PC-DOS, contains a set of programs often known as "utilities" that help you to organise your PC efficiently. Although a lot of these are only of use to the computer scientist a number of them can be of great value to the anyone who uses a spreadsheet. A short description of these now follows. Each of these programs is set into motion by typing the name given in heavy type. Take note of the layout of each command and make sure that it is copied exactly. The position of the spaces is critical. You must make sure that you type the command as it is given to you and not what you think it ought to be! End every command by pressing the RETURN (Enter) key. This is the key that says, "Over to you".

DIR This is the program that gives a list of every file stored on a specified disk. It will list the name of the file, the number of bytes (characters) it contains, its date of creation and the time of creation. In addition it will tell you how much space is left on the disk.

A>**DIR** will list all the files on the disk in drive A, as shown in Figure 1.5.

Fig 1.5 *Directory listing*

Directory of A:\

CASHFLOW	62600	21-10-87	17:26
PARAINV	1337	1-01-80	0:23
ALTM MAC	10	15-10-87	9:37
ALTA MAC	16	15-10-87	9:47
ALTC MAC	26	15-10-87	9:53
QREF1 BK!	4895	15-10-87	10:03
QREF	4898	15-10-87	10:21
BOX	950	15-10-87	12:05
JOTEST 001	767	1-01-87	0:31
LIST	379	15-10-87	12:36
JOTEST1 001	190	1-01-87	0:20
BSLET1 CAL	198	1-01-87	0:25
JOTEST1 CAL	98	1-01-87	0:32
WP9JO BK!	57268	20-10-87	15:44
JO CAL	98	1-01-87	0:45
JOTEST CAL	98	1-01-87	0:47
WP9JO	63266	20-10-87	1:36
PAGINATE	1475	1-01-87	1:51
WP3	25567	22-10-87	11:47

19 File(s)   126976 bytes free

A>**DIR B:** will list every file on the disk in drive B.

A>**DIR/P** will display the file list, but a page at a time. This is because it is possible that there may be so many files on the disk that their names will occupy more than the twenty four lines of the screen. This amendment to the command will allow you to read the file list at your leisure.

You will probably notice that most file names are followed by a three letter "extension". This extension tells us something about the type of file it is. A file name followed by DOC or TXT would be a document or a text file, one followed by EXE or COM are program files. File names can consist of a combination of no more than eight letters and numbers. Spreadsheets tend to have extensions that reflect the program generating them: WKS is a Lotus worksheet, CAL is a SuperCalc sheet and LGX is a Logistix worksheet. A complete file name will consist of three parts: the drive on which it is currently located, its name and its extension. The drive name is separated from the name by a colon, : , and the file name is separated from the extension by a fullstop (period). Hence the name

A:JOB1.CAL

refers to a file called JOB1 on the disk in drive A which has a CAL extension (sometimes referred to a "dot CAL" extension), telling us that it is a document. If there is no drive name prefixing the file name it is assumed to be on the logged disk drive.
You can use "wildcards" in file names. These are the characters ? and *. By using wildcard characters you can list, for example, all the SuperCalc files on the disk in drive A by the command

A>DIR *.CAL

as shown in Figure 1.6.

Fig 1.6 *Listing of all the .CAL files*

```
Directory of  A:\


BSLET1   CAL      198    1-01-87    0:25
JOTEST1  CAL       98    1-01-87    0:32
JO       CAL       98    1-01-87    0:45


         3 File(s)        126976 bytes free
```

All the files on drive B that start with the letters TH are listed by the command

A>DIR B:TH*.*

If you want to list all the files that are five characters long and can have anything in the first three places but must have the number 86 following them you can use the command

A>DIR ???86.*

The ? character stands for a single character, but * stands for any number of characters. This system of wildcards is also used in the COPY and DEL instructions that are detailed later in this section.

FORMAT This will allow you to prepare a blank floppy disk to receive saved documents. If you have a twin floppy disk system the instruction is issued with the master operating system disk in drive A and a blank disk in drive B. The instruction is then

A>FORMAT B :

Formatting a disk will wipe everything off the disk if you happen to be using a disk which already has files stored on it. This is perfectly all right if you have nothing on the disk you wish to keep. Thus you can re-use disks containing out-of-date documents. Early versions of DOS will always assume that the current drive is meant if no drive name is specified. This could result in your reformatting the DOS disk. Not something you normally would wish to do! Luckily, the latest versions of the operating system do not allow you to make that mistake.

COPY This allows you to take a copy of a file and place it on another disk. (Or you can make a copy of a file on the same disk provided the copy has a different name from the original.)

A>COPY JOB1.CAL B:

will place a copy of the file called JOB1.CAL on the disk in drive A on to the disk in drive B.

A>COPY JOB1.CAL B:JOB2.CAL

will place a copy of the file called JOB1.CAL on the

disk in drive A on to the disk in drive B, but this time the copy will be called JOB2.CAL. The instruction to copy a set of files from one disk to another could look like this

A>COPY *.CAL B :

which would all the files with a CAL extension on the disk in drive A on to the disk in drive B.

DISKCOPY This command will allow you to make an identical copy of one floppy disk on to another. **DISKCOPY** formats the "target" disk before copying takes place. The command looks like this

A>DISKCOPY A : B :

which tells the operating system to make a copy of the disk in drive A on to the disk in drive B. The way to do it is to ensure that the operating system disk is in drive A before issuing the command. You will then be told to place the "source" disk in drive A and the "target" disk in drive B. This means that you have to remove the master operating system disk and then replace it with the disk to be copied.

DEL This command will erase a file from a disk. Once deleted a file cannot normally be recovered. In order to delete, for example, all the files from the disk in drive A that have CAL extensions

A>DEL *.CAL

will delete all CAL files from drive A and

A>DEL B : *.CAL

will delete all CAL files from the disk in drive B. Beware, unless you really mean to do it, of the command

A>DEL *.*

Luckily the operating system will query you by asking

Are you Sure? (Y/N)

since if you answer "Y" for "Yes" this command will delete every file on the disk irrespective of its name and extension.

1.5 INSTALLING A SPREADSHEET PROGRAM

When you purchase a spreadsheet program you will receive one or more program disks and a bulky manual. The disks contain the program files and very often a disk of example worksheets. The manual accompanying these programs is usually fairly hefty and you might be put off by its size and complexity. This is one of the reasons why this book has been written. These manuals are all very well and are extremely useful if you know what to look for in them. The newcomer to this type of program needs to know just what it is capable of doing for him. Spreadsheet programs can be described as solutions looking for problems to solve. Once you become aware of the wide range of problems whose solution lies in a spreadsheet you are going to be able to use the full power of the program.

The first thing you must do is to read the instructions at the start of the manual to find out how to install the program for use on your machine. If you have a machine with twin floppy disks then you need to make working copies of the disks and store the originals away. The usual way to make copies is to use the DOS command **COPY**, as described earlier in this chapter. However, some programs use disks are copy-protected. The Lotus 1-2-3 program is a case in point. The main program disk is prepared in such a way as to prevent copying taking place. This prevents illegal distribution of the program. Hence you are provided with two copies of the master disk and one of these must always be in drive A while the program is running. If you have a hard disk system you are able to copy the program files on to the hard disk and a special program is supplied to allow you to do this. When this operation takes place the original disk is modified so that the copying cannot take place again. By doing this the program can be run without a master disk in the floppy disk drive.

Most spreadsheets have an INSTALL program that tells the program what type of computer it is running on and what printer and, possibly, plotter are being used. This is necessary because many of the spreadsheet programs plot graphs and in order to do this have to know the characteristics of the screen they are to be displayed on and the device they are to be printed on.

1.6 KEEPING TRACK OF FILES

This section applies particularly to those users who have a PC with a hard disk drive. Hard disk drives can store several hundred files, but by virtue of this, and our natural reluctance to get rid of anything if we do not really need to, it becomes quite a task to keep track of what we have got. Two rules that can be used by both hard disk and floppy disk systems are:

1. Keep program files and worksheets separate from each other.

2. Devise a naming system so that you can easily identify a worksheet from its name.

The first rule is fairly easy to apply if you have a twin floppy disk system. It is to keep the program disk in drive A; this is usually not difficult to do as most systems force you to do it. Additionally you should make sure that you never store any worksheets on this disk. Always ensure that worksheets are saved on the disk currently in drive B. This then makes it easy to store the worksheets in groups by allocating specific disks to particular types of worksheets.

If you have a hard disk system you can approach the problem in several ways. It relies on the fact that you divide the disk up into a series of sub-directories. This splits the storage areas up into parts, one of which can be allocated to a wordprocessing program, another part to an accounting program, another to a spreadsheet program and so on. If your disk has no sub-directories every time you issue the command

C>**DIR**

you will get a list of files stored in the "root", or main, directory. However, you can organise your disk in a tree-like structure so that leading from this root are a series of "branches" as shown in Figure 1.7

Fig 1.7 *Directory organisation*

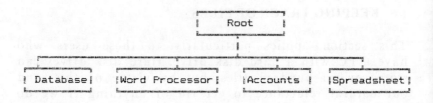

In order to create a sub-directory the command **MD** or **MKDIR** (Make Directory) is used. For example

C>MD SS

In order to get into that part of the disk now you have to use the command **CD** or **CHDIR**, (Change Directory). For example

C>CD \SS

and you will be moved into the new directory, which, if you use the **DIR** command now will be seen to be empty. Note the \, backslash character, that separates the command from the name of the new sub-directory. In order to return to the root directory all you need is the command

**C>CD **

It is very easy to copy files into this directory from a floppy disk by going into the directory, using **CD \SS**, and then using the command

C>COPY A:*.*

This will then copy all the files from the floppy disk in drive A into that sub-directory. Alternatively, the spreadsheet manual supplied with your software may tell you exactly how to set up the program to run from a hard disk.

Every time you wish to use the spreadsheet you can enter that directory and ensure that all the worksheets you create and edit are kept on a disk in the floppy disk drive. Alternatively, if your spreadsheet allows you to do so, you could keep your worksheet in yet another sub-directory on your hard disk well out of the way of accounts files and other irrelevant material. Try always to use a name relevant to the worksheet you are saving. To use names such as SHEET1, SHEET2 etc makes it very difficult to identify the job performed by the worksheet. If you use a more meaningful naming system you will have a better chance of keeping track of everything. For example, remembering that you have eight characters available for every file name. So long as the system is consistent and simple, then you will have few problems. A dairy company known to the author uses a spreadsheet program and saves its worksheets with names such as FRUITYOG, MILKSALE, ROUND1 and so on.

SUMMARY

1. Your PC consists of a screen, a keyboard, a system box and a printer.
2. The system box contains the computer, the memory and either two floppy disk drives or a hard disk and a single floppy disk.
3. Floppy disks are removable but store far fewer documents than hard disks. The disks are used for long term storage of documents.
4. The important keys on the keyboard are **Ctrl**, **Alt** **Return/Enter** and **Esc**. Many spreadsheets use the ten F (Function) keys as well.
5. Load the operating system into the computer's memory before loading the spreadsheet program.
6. Always make a copy of the master disks supplied for your spreadsheet, unless the disks are protected against copying.
7. Use the copies to install the system and for day-to-day running, unless you have to use copy-protected disks.

8. Follow the supplier's instructions in order to install your spreadsheet correctly so that it can use your equipment, particularly the printer, efficiently.

9. Printers can be dot matrix, for fast medium quality or slow high quality printing and daisywheel for high quality printing.

10. A plotter is a dedicated output device used for drawing graphs.

11. The important operating system commands are DIR, COPY, DISKCOPY, MD, CD, FORMAT and DEL.

12. Files can have names made from up to eight characters and an optional three character extension.

13. For economy of space divide your hard disk up into a series of sub-directories.

14. Always keep worksheet document files and program files on disks in different drives or in different directories.

BASIC SPREADSHEET
CONCEPTS

This chapter explains and illustrates the way a spreadsheet works so that you can begin to see what is behind the concept and how it can be used to your advantage.

2.1 LOADING YOUR SPREADSHEET PROGRAM

After you have gone through the procedure of "booting up" your computer you will see either a A> (floppy disk system) or a C> (hard disk system) displayed on the screen. This is the operating system prompt telling you that it is waiting for you to give it an instruction. If you have a floppy disk machine remove the operating system disk and replace it with the master spreadsheet program disk. Place your disk to contain the worksheets into drive B and start the spreadsheet program. This will be a short code word such as

A>lotus

for Lotus 1-2-3

A>SC3

for SuperCalc3

or

A>lgx

for Logistix

You will then usually get a copyright notice screen which will eventually be replaced with a screen that ~

looks similar to that shown in Figure 2.1. This screen, in fact, is the one produced by the Lotus 1-2-3 program, but they are all very similar.

Fig 2.1 *Lotus 1-2-3 screen*

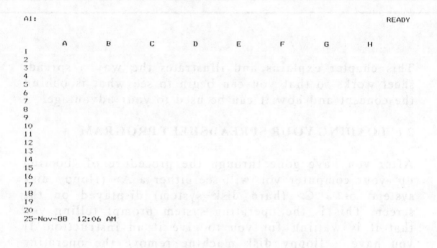

The first thing you should notice is that the screen is now divided up into a series of "cells" and that the cell in the top left hand corner is illuminated by the cursor. Each cell is identified by reference to its row and column in the form of a "map reference". Most, but not all, spreadsheets use letters of the alphabet to name columns and numbers to identify the rows. The top left hand cell is known as A1 in our illustration. What you are seeing, in fact, is only a small portion of a very large sheet with possibly hundreds of columns and thousands of rows. The naming of columns goes from A to Z, then AA to AZ, BA to BZ and possibly up to IV. You will see the reference of the current cell, in our example, at the top left-hand corner of the screen.

Anything you now type will now appear beside the cell reference. This is your way in to the worksheet. You may type a number, a word or a formula at this point and when you have pressed the **Return** (**Enter**) key that number, word or formula is then "written" on to the current cell. The result of typing the word "Stock" followed by Return is shown in Figure 2.2. Notice how the contents of the current cell are now displayed beside the cell reference. It should perhaps be noted at this point that some spreadsheets have the entry information displayed at the bottom of the screen.

Fig 2.2 *Text entry on to sheet*

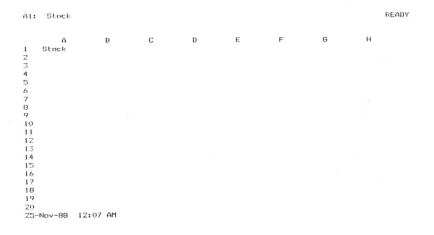

2.2 MOVING ABOUT YOUR SPREADSHEET

The four arrow keys on the keypad on the right of your keyboard are used to move the cursor about your spreadsheet. The cursor will move in the direction shown on the arrow key. If the cursor reaches one of the edges of the sheet and you try to move it further in that direction the program will cause the computer to emit a loud "beep"! If you reach a position a long way from cell A1, as shown in Figure 2.3 then you can usually return to A1 by pressing the key marked "Home".

Fig 2.3 *The extreme edge of a spreadsheet*

```
IV8192:                                                        READY

          IO      IP      IQ      IR      IS      IT      IU      IV
8173
8174
8175
8176
8177
8178
8179
8180
8181
8182
8183
8184
8185
8186
8187
8188
8189
8190
8191
8192
25-Nov-88  12:08 AM
```

In addition you can move to any cell in the sheet by pressing a special key that is the "GoTo" key; it varies from program to program. On pressing this key you will get a message saying, for example

GoTo where?

and you respond by entering the cell reference you wish to go to. On pressing Return the cursor goes to that cell at once and you are moved to another part of the sheet.

Very often, by using combinations of keys, you can move in any direction by one screenful.

2.3 TYPES OF SPREADSHEET ENTRIES

In simple terms there are three types of entry you can make into a spreadsheet. These are

1. Numbers

2. Text, i.e. words

3. Formulas

Numbers provide the data which is manipulated on the worksheet; spreadsheets are "number crunchers" in the same way that word processors are "word crunchers". Text entries are used to add information about the nature of the entries contained in your worksheet. Finally the formulas that you enter tell the program what to do to the numbers you have entered. For example a formula will say "multiply the number in cell A3 by the number in cell C3 and add to it 10 times the number in cell D4". The answer always appears in the cell containing the formula.

Spreadsheet programs generally detect the difference between these types of entries in one of two ways. The first of these is the program that takes its cue from the first character you enter. If that character is a letter of the alphabet then it assumes that what follows is going to be text. If the first character is a digit (0 to 9), a plus or a minus sign or a left hand bracket then what follows is bound to be a number or a formula that will result in display of a number. Lotus 1-2-3 works like this and Figures 2.4 and 2.5 show the result of such entries being made. The entry causes an indicator in the top right-hand corner of the Lotus screen to show the type of entry. Text is known as a "LABEL" and a number or a formula is known as a "VALUE". This means that the formula to add the contents of D3 to the contents of E3 must be entered as

+D3+E3

The other way that the program identifies the type of entry is by waiting until the entry is complete and then scanning it to see if it appears to be text, a number or a formula. In certain cases you need to tell the program that what appears to be a number entry is in fact a text entry by starting the entry with a single or double quotation mark. For example, if you want to enter a date

Fig 2.4 *Numerical entry on sheet*

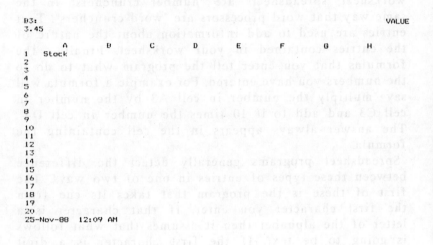

Fig 2.5 *Formula entered on to sheet*

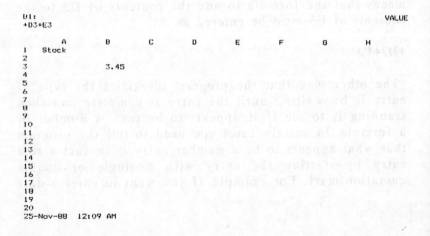

such as

12/4/87

then because the / sign is used to indicate division the entry will appear as

.0344827

unless the entry is actually made as

"12/4/87

You will usually find that although you enter text without a leading quotation mark the program will automatically insert one for you. This is how it keeps track internally of the different types of entry.

If a formula is entered incorrectly, usually by having unmatched brackets, then a spreadsheet program will usually interpret the entry as being text and display it a such. In this case there are editing facilities available in all the spreadsheet programs that enable you to add or remove the offending brackets allowing you to try again. If you do this, however, you should make sure that you get rid of the quotation mark placed in front of the expression by the program.

It is important to take note of the following fact, the reason for which will become clear shortly. It is that although you might have the cursor at cell reference A4 and you enter the formula

+A2+D2

as shown in Figure 2.6 what is actually stored is

"add the contents of the cell two rows above me in this column to the contents of the cell two rows above me in the column three to the right of me".

28

Fig 2.6 *Calculation of formula*

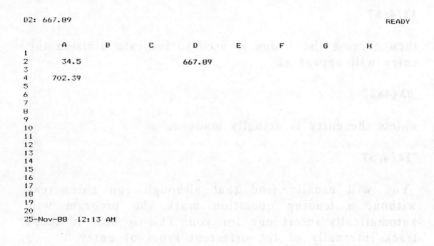

```
D2: 667.89                                              READY

        A       B       C       D       E       F       G       H
1
2      34.5                    667.89
3
4     702.39
5
6
7
8
9
10
11
12
13
14
15
16
17
18
19
20
25-Nov-88  12:13 AM
```

The spreadsheet program called Multiplan actually uses this type of cell referencing and the same entry is shown in Figure 2.7 on a Multiplan screen.

Fig 2.7 *Multiplan screen*

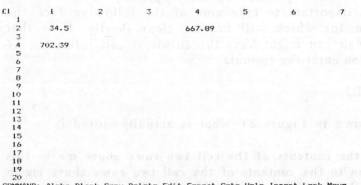

```
£1          1       2       3       4       5       6       7
1
2          34.5                    667.89
3
4         702.39
5
6
7
8
9
10
11
12
13
14
15
16
17
18
19
20
COMMAND: Alpha Blank Copy Delete Edit Format Goto Help Insert Lock Move
         Name Options Print Quit Run Sort Transfer Value Window Xternal
Select   option or type command letter
R4C1        +R[-2]C+R[-2]C[+3]           100% Free     Multiplan: TEMP
```

2.4 SPREADSHEET COMMANDS

As well as entering data on to the spreadsheet you can enter commands that enable you to alter the layout of the sheet, print it, save it away and even change the way that the spreadsheet program works. Most, but not all, spreadsheet programs provide you with a list of options after you have pressed the / key. This is a carry over from the days of the very first spreadsheet program called VisiCalc and all the programs now available are modelled to some extent on this program. Three typical command lines are shown in Figures 2.8, 2.9.1, 2.9.2 and 2.10. They are the command lines from Lotus 1-2-3, SuperCalc and Multiplan. The Lotus command line lists the options available with a further menu of options available beneath the one highlighted. In this case the cursor is on the first option controlling operations that can be carried out by selecting the **Worksheet** option.

In the second example, taken from SuperCalc, the options are listed by their initial letters. Selecting one of these, by pressing the appropriate letter key, displays the entire command and follows this by the detailed command instructions - Figures 2.9.1 and 2.9.2.

With Multiplan the options are always displayed and do not need to be called up by pressing a special key. An option is selected by pressing the key corresponding to its initial letter.

2.5 CREATING A SIMPLE SPREADSHEET

What follows next details the steps that need to be taken in order to create a simple spreadsheet. The example is that of a stock list of items in a hardware store. For this we need to know the part number of each item, its description, the number in stock, the cost price and the selling price. From this information we can calculate the total value of the stock. For the purpose of this example the SuperCalc spreadsheet program has been chosen, but the steps taken will be the same whatever program is used.

30

Fig 2.8 *Lotus options*

```
A1: U 'Glendale Hardware Ltd
Worksheet  Range  Copy  Move  File  Print  Graph  Data  System  Quit
Global, Insert, Delete, Column, Erase, Titles, Window, Status, Page
       A        B       C        D        E        F        G        H
 1  Glendale Hardware Ltd
 2
 3  Rate of exchange:    1.56 $/#
 4  Sea Freight :        0.54 #/kilo
 5  Air Freight :        1.21 #/kilo
 6
 7  Item     Weight/kgPrice - $Price - #Cost - # Cost - #
 8                                      Sea      Air
 9  ADO16         40        67 42.94871 64.54871 91.34871
10  ADO17         23        55 35.25641 47.67641 63.08641
11  ADO18         12        34 21.79487 28.27487 36.31487
12  PDO89         45        78    .50      74.3   104.45
13  PDO90         43        89 57.05128 80.27128 109.0812
14  PDO99         31        90 57.69230 74.43230 95.20230
15  JTO67        100       340 217.9487 271.9487 338.9487
16  JTO68        122       400 256.4102 322.2902 404.0302
17  JTO70        160       450 288.4615 374.8615 482.0615
18  JTO98        180       500 320.5128 417.7128 538.3128
19
20
11-May-88   12:41 PM
```

Fig 2.9.1 *SuperCalc options*

```
      |  A  ||  B  ||  C  ||  D  ||  E  ||  F  ||  G  ||  H  |
 1
 2
 3
 4
 5
 6
 7
 8
 9
10
11
12
13
14
15
16
17
18
19
20
> A1
Enter A,B,C,D,E,F,G,I,L,M,O,P,Q,R,S,T,U,V,W,X,Z,/,?
  2>/
F1 = Help; F2 = Erase Line/Return to Spreadsheet; F9 = Plot; F10 = View
```

Fig 2.9.2 *SuperCalc sub-menu*

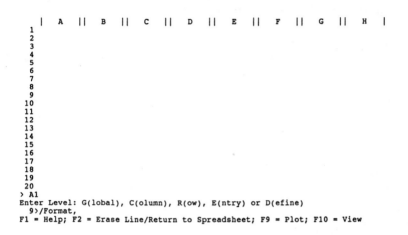

```
    |  A  ||  B  ||  C  ||  D  ||  E  ||  F  ||  G  ||  H  |
 1
 2
 3
 4
 5
 6
 7
 8
 9
10
11
12
13
14
15
16
17
18
19
20
> A1
Enter Level: G(lobal), C(olumn), R(ow), E(ntry) or D(efine)
  9>/Format,
F1 = Help; F2 = Erase Line/Return to Spreadsheet; F9 = Plot; F10 = View
```

Fig 2.10 *Multiplan option line*

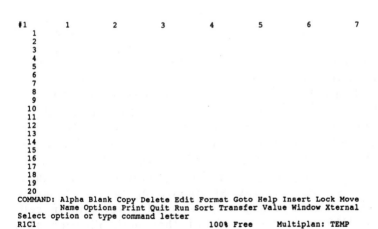

```
#1      1      2      3      4      5      6      7
 1
 2
 3
 4
 5
 6
 7
 8
 9
10
11
12
13
14
15
16
17
18
19
20
COMMAND: Alpha Blank Copy Delete Edit Format Goto Help Insert Lock Move
         Name Options Print Quit Run Sort Transfer Value Window Xternal
Select option or type command letter
R1C1                              100% Free      Multiplan: TEMP
```

First of all the headings of the columns are entered. Then the stock reference, the description and the size of each stock item are entered in the first three columns, as shown in Figure 2.11.

Fig 2.11 *Stock sheet*

```
A1: U 'Ref.                                                        READY

        A          B          C       D    E    F    G    H
 1   Ref.       Descr.     Size
 2   1234       Bolts      1/2 inch
 3   2314       Bolts      1/4 inch
 4   3217       Bolts      1/8 inch
 5   3425       Nuts       1/2 inch
 6   3456       Nuts       1/4 inch
 7   4522       Nuts       1/8 inch
 8   4542       Screws     No. 8
 9   6564       Screws     No. 6
10   6755       Screws     No. 4
11   6757       Screws     No. 2
12   6767       Locks      2 Lever
13   6777       Locks      4 Lever
14   6888       Spanners   14 mm
15   7865       Spanners   16 mm
16   9876       Spanners   18 mm
17
18
19
20
25-Nov-88   12:01 AM
```

The number currently in stock for each item is entered in column D with the corresponding cost price, in pounds and decimals of a pound, in column E. Next the selling price, similarly in pounds and decimals of a pound, are entered in column F. These are shown in Figure 2.12. Column H contains the value of each stock item and this is found by multiplying the entry in column D by the corresponding entry in column E. This means that in cell H2 there is the formula D2*E2. In cell H3 there is the formula D3*E3, and so on. You should note that the * symbol is used for the arithmetic operation of multiplication. Although you have entered a formula in cells H3 to H16 it is the result of that multiplication that is displayed. There are ways and means of displaying formulas, but that will be covered later. The worksheet now looks as shown in Figure 2.13. Finally we need to be able to find the grand total of the values of all the stock items and the result is as shown in Figure 2.14.

Fig 2.12 *Stock sheet (continued)*

```
A1: U 'Ref.                                                    READY

     A          B          C          D       E        F          G        H
 1   Ref.       Descr.     Size       In stock Cost     Selling Price
 2   1234       Bolts      1/2 inch   200      0.78     1.04
 3   2314       Bolts      1/4 inch   240      0.55     0.73
 4   3217       Bolts      1/8 inch   480      0.46     0.61
 5   3425       Nuts       1/2 inch   198      0.21     0.28
 6   3456       Nuts       1/4 inch   188      0.15     0.21
 7   4522       Nuts       1/8 inch   500      0.12     0.16
 8   4542       Screws     No. 8      3450     0.05     0.07
 9   6564       Screws     No. 6      2490     0.04     0.05
10   6755       Screws     No. 4      1250     0.03     0.04
11   6757       Screws     No. 2      4320     0.02     0.03
12   6767       Locks      2 Lever    56       4.78     6.36
13   6777       Locks      4 Lever    43       7.88     10.48
14   6888       Spanners   14 mm      100      1.22     1.62
15   7865       Spanners   16 mm      95       1.45     1.93
16   9876       Spanners   18 mm      66       1.78     2.37
17
18
19
20
25-Nov-88   12:02 AM
```

Fig 2.13 *Stock sheet (continued)*

```
A1: U 'Ref.                                                    READY

     A          B          C          D       E        F          G        H
 1   Ref.       Descr.     Size       In stock Cost     Selling Price      Value
 2   1234       Bolts      1/2 inch   200      0.78     1.04               156
 3   2314       Bolts      1/4 inch   240      0.55     0.73               132
 4   3217       Bolts      1/8 inch   480      0.46     0.61               220.8
 5   3425       Nuts       1/2 inch   198      0.21     0.28               41.58
 6   3456       Nuts       1/4 inch   188      0.15     0.21               28.2
 7   4522       Nuts       1/8 inch   500      0.12     0.16               60
 8   4542       Screws     No. 8      3450     0.05     0.07               172.5
 9   6564       Screws     No. 6      2490     0.04     0.05               99.6
10   6755       Screws     No. 4      1250     0.03     0.04               37.5
11   6757       Screws     No. 2      4320     0.02     0.03               86.4
12   6767       Locks      2 Lever    56       4.78     6.36               267.68
13   6777       Locks      4 Lever    43       7.88     10.48              338.84
14   6888       Spanners   14 mm      100      1.22     1.62               122
15   7865       Spanners   16 mm      95       1.45     1.93               137.75
16   9876       Spanners   18 mm      66       1.78     2.37               117.48
17
18
19
20
25-Nov-88   12:03 AM
```

Fig 2.14 *Stock sheet finally*

	A	B	C	D	E	F	G	H
1	Ref.	Descr.	Size	In stock	Cost	Selling Price		Value
2	1234	Bolts	1/2 inch	200	0.78	1.04		156
3	2314	Bolts	1/4 inch	240	0.55	0.73		132
4	3217	Bolts	1/8 inch	480	0.46	0.61		220.8
5	3425	Nuts	1/2 inch	198	0.21	0.28		41.58
6	3456	Nuts	1/4 inch	188	0.15	0.21		28.2
7	4522	Nuts	1/8 inch	500	0.12	0.16		60
8	4542	Screws	No. 8	3450	0.05	0.07		172.5
9	6564	Screws	No. 6	2490	0.04	0.05		99.6
10	6755	Screws	No. 4	1250	0.03	0.04		37.5
11	6757	Screws	No. 2	4320	0.02	0.03		86.4
12	6767	Locks	2 Lever	56	4.78	6.36		267.68
13	6777	Locks	4 Lever	43	7.88	10.48		338.84
14	6888	Spanners	14 mm	100	1.22	1.62		122
15	7865	Spanners	16 mm	95	1.45	1.93		137.75
16	9876	Spanners	18 mm	66	1.78	2.37		117.48
17							Total	2018.33
18								
19								
20								

25-Nov-88   12:06 AM

This grand total can be calculated in one of two ways. The most obvious is to say that the figure in cell H17 is found by entering the formula

H2+H3+H4+H5+H6+H7+H8+H9+H10+H11+H12+H13+H14·+H15+H16

but this seems to be a rather tedious way of doing things. As you might expect, there is a simpler way that is used by all spreadsheet programs. It employs using a spreadsheet **function**. This is a feature that says "add up all the cells in the following range" and it looks generally like this:

sum(h2:h16)

where the keyword is the word **sum** and the range to be summed is enclosed within the brackets separated, in this case, by a colon (:) character. All spreadsheets use a function of this form. There are many of these functions that make easy work of many complicated calculations.

2.6 SAVING AND PRINTING

Having decided that your worksheet is complete you will almost certainly wish to preserve it for future use and reference. A simple command can be used to save the worksheet on to a disk, the one in drive B if you are using a twin floppy disk system, and your worksheet is saved away in a form such that it can be worked on again at a later date. If you are using a hard disk system you still need to save your worksheets on to floppy disks. Such saving will attach a special extension on to the filename to ensure that it can be read back again by the program that created it. It is possible, however, that worksheets can be read by other spreadsheet programs. It is particularly easy, for example, for the Logistix program to read sheets created by Lotus and SuperCalc.

Finally you will need to print out your finished worksheet and the result of this is shown in Figure 2.15. You should notice that only the spreadsheet display is printed and row and column labels are omitted.

Fig 2.15 *Printout from spreadsheet*

Ref.	Descr.	Size	In stock	Cost	Selling Price	Value
1234	Bolts	1/2 inch	200	0.78	1.04	156
2314	Bolts	1/4 inch	240	0.55	0.73	132
3217	Bolts	1/8 inch	480	0.46	0.61	220.8
3425	Nuts	1/2 inch	198	0.21	0.28	41.58
3456	Nuts	1/4 inch	188	0.15	0.21	28.2
4522	Nuts	1/8 inch	500	0.12	0.16	60
4542	Screws	No. 8	3450	0.05	0.07	172.5
6564	Screws	No. 6	2490	0.04	0.05	99.6
6755	Screws	No. 4	1250	0.03	0.04	37.5
6757	Screws	No. 2	4320	0.02	0.03	86.4
6767	Locks	2 Lever	56	4.78	6.36	267.68
6777	Locks	4 Lever	43	7.88	10.48	338.84
6888	Spanners	14 mm	100	1.22	1.62	122
7865	Spanners	16 mm	95	1.45	1.93	137.75
9876	Spanners	18 mm	66	1.78	2.37	117.48
					Total	2018.33

If you wish you can list the contents of each cell in your worksheet so that you obtain a listing as shown in Figure 2.16.

Fig 2.16 *Listing of spreadsheet contents*

A1: U 'Ref.	F6: U 0.21	D12: U 56
B1: U 'Descr.	H6: U +E6*D6	E12: U 4.78
C1: U 'Size	A7: U '4522	F12: U 6.36
D1: U 'In stock	B7: U 'Nuts	H12: U +E12*D12
E1: U 'Cost	C7: U '1/8 inch	A13: U '6777
F1: U 'Selling Price	D7: U 500	B13: U 'Locks
H1: U 'Value	E7: U 0.12	C13: U '4 Lever
A2: U '1234	F7: U 0.16	D13: U 43
B2: U 'Bolts	H7: U +E7*D7	E13: U 7.88
C2: U '1/2 inch	A8: U '4542	F13: U 10.48
D2: U 200	B8: U 'Screws	H13: U +E13*D13
E2: U 0.78	C8: U 'No. 8	A14: U '6888
F2: U 1.04	D8: U 3450	B14: U 'Spanners
H2: U +E2*D2	E8: U 0.05	C14: U '14 mm
A3: U '2314	F8: U 0.07	D14: U 100
B3: U 'Bolts	H8: U +E8*D8	E14: U 1.22
C3: U '1/4 inch	A9: U '6564	F14: U 1.62
D3: U 240	B9: U 'Screws	H14: U +E14*D14
E3: U 0.55	C9: U 'No. 6	A15: U '7865
F3: U 0.73	D9: U 2490	B15: U 'Spanners
H3: U +E3*D3	E9: U 0.04	C15: U '16 mm
A4: U '3217	F9: U 0.05	D15: U 95
B4: U 'Bolts	H9: U +E9*D9	E15: U 1.45
C4: U '1/8 inch	A10: U '6755	F15: U 1.93
D4: U 480	B10: U 'Screws	H15: U +E15*D15
E4: U 0.46	C10: U 'No. 4	A16: U '9876
F4: U 0.61	D10: U 1250	B16: U 'Spanners
H4: U +E4*D4	E10: U 0.03	C16: U '18 mm
A5: U '3425	F10: U 0.04	D16: U 66
B5: U 'Nuts	H10: U +E10*D10	E16: U 1.78
C5: U '1/2 inch	A11: U '6757	F16: U 2.37
D5: U 198	B11: U 'Screws	H16: U +E16*D16
E5: U 0.21	C11: U 'No. 2	G17: U 'Total
F5: U 0.28	D11: U 4320	H17: U @SUM(H16..H2)
H5: U +E5*D5	E11: U 0.02	
A6: U '3456	F11: U 0.03	
B6: U 'Nuts	H11: U +E11*D11	
C6: U '1/4 inch	A12: U '6767	
D6: U 188	B12: U 'Locks	
E6: U 0.15	C12: U '2 Lever	

2.7 THE "WHAT-IF" CONCEPT

Once your worksheet has been created if is very easy to put it to work for you. For example if, in our example, items were put into stock or taken out of stock. A stock list never stays static and so the total value of the stock varies from day to day and possibly even from hour to hour. The great value of spreadsheets is that if you change any one number on the sheet the whole sheet can be recalculated immediately. This means that if we put another 1000 1/8 inch bolts into stock and three 2 lever locks sold then the new value of the stock can be discovered as soon as those entries were made, giving the result shown in Figure 2.17.

This concept can be shown in another example. In this one a company imports goods from the USA and so their prices depend on the rate of exchange. In addition, the final price is also dependent on another variable which is the method of freighting used. Air freight costs more than sea freight and so the final cost to the importer depends on two independent variables. On the screen the worksheet looks as shown in Figure 2.18.

Fig 2.17 *Revised stock sheet*

D12: U 53

	A	B	C	D	E	F	G	H
1	Ref.	Descr.	Size	In stock	Cost	Selling Price		Value
2	1234	Bolts	1/2 inch	200	0.78	1.04		156
3	2314	Bolts	1/4 inch	240	0.55	0.73		132
4	3217	Bolts	1/8 inch	1480	0.46	0.61		680.8
5	3425	Nuts	1/2 inch	198	0.21	0.28		41.58
6	3456	Nuts	1/4 inch	188	0.15	0.21		28.2
7	4522	Nuts	1/8 inch	500	0.12	0.16		60
8	4542	Screws	No. 8	3450	0.05	0.07		172.5
9	6564	Screws	No. 6	2490	0.04	0.05		99.6
10	6755	Screws	No. 4	1250	0.03	0.04		37.5
11	6757	Screws	No. 2	4320	0.02	0.03		86.4
12	6767	Locks	2 Lever	53	4.78	6.36		253.34
13	6777	Locks	4 Lever	43	7.88	10.48		338.84
14	6888	Spanners	14 mm	100	1.22	1.62		122
15	7865	Spanners	16 mm	95	1.45	1.93		137.75
16	9876	Spanners	18 mm	66	1.78	2.37		117.48
17							Total	2463.99
18								
19								
20								

11-May-88   12:34 PM

Fig 2.18 *Freight costs*

```
A1: U 'Glendale Hardware Ltd                                    READY

         A          B           C         D        E        F         G      H
 1   Glendale Hardware Ltd
 2
 3   Rate of exchange:        1.76 $/£
 4   Sea Freight :            0.45 £/kilo
 5   Air Freight :            1.25 £/kilo
 6
 7   Item        Weight/kgPrice - $Price - £Cost - £ Cost - £
 8                                          Sea      Air
 9   ADO16           40        67 38.06818 56.06818 88.06818
10   ADO17           23        55   31.25    41.6     60
11   ADO18           12        34 19.31818 24.71818 34.31818
12   PDO89           45        78 44.31818 64.56818 100.5681
13   PDO90           43        89 50.56818 69.91818 104.3181
14   PDO99           31        90 51.13636 65.08636 89.88636
15   JTO67          100       340 193.1818 238.1818 318.1818
16   JTO68          122       400 227.2727 282.1727 379.7727
17   JTO70          160       450 255.6818 327.6818 455.6818
18   JTO98          180       500 284.0909 365.0909 509.0909
19
20
25-Nov-88   12:10 AM
```

The whole sheet can change considerably if all three variables, the rate of exchange, the cost of sea freight and the cost of air freight alter. The result is shown in Figure 2.19. The sheet is so constructed as to tie the costs to the three things that are variable and these are arranged at the top of the sheet. Change any one of these and the whole sheet changes. The actual contents of the sheet are shown in Figure 2.20. You should notice that the entries in the range D9 to D18 are all calculated by dividing the number in the column to the left of each entry by the number held in cell C3 in order to calculate the cost in pounds sterling. The entries in the cells in the block E9 to F18 are all tied to the entries in their row and to the freight charges in either C4 or C5 depending on whether the freight charge is for air or sea.

This example gives an indication of the power of a spreadsheet program. It enables you to indulge in the luxury of playing the "what if I" game. This is far easier to do than spending hours with a pencil, paper and calculator with the possibility, even then, of errors.

Fig 2.19 *Revised freight costs*

```
A1: U 'Glendale Hardware Ltd                                      READY

     A        B          C        D       E        F       G       H
1   Glendale Hardware Ltd
2
3   Rate of exchange:    1.56 $/£
4   Sea Freight :        0.54 £/kilo
5   Air Freight :        1.21 £/kilo
6
7   Item       Weight/kgPrice - $Price - £Cost - £ Cost - £
8                                             Sea      Air
9   AD016          40      67 42.94871 64.54871 91.34871
10  AD017          23      55 35.25641 47.67641 63.08641
11  AD018          12      34 21.79487 28.27487 36.31487
12  PD089          45      78       50     74.3   104.45
13  PD090          43      89 57.05128 80.27128 109.0812
14  PD099          31      90 57.69230 74.43230 95.20230
15  JT067         100     340 217.9487 271.9487 338.9487
16  JT068         122     400 256.4102 322.2902 404.0302
17  JT070         160     450 288.4615 374.8615 482.0615
18  JT098         180     500 320.5128 417.7128 538.3128
19
20
25-Nov-88  12:11 AM
```

Fig 2.20 *Contents of freight cost sheet*

A1: U 'Glendale Hardware Ltd
A3: U 'Rate of exchange:
C3: U 1.56
D3: U '$/#
A4: U 'Sea Freight :
C4: U 0.54
D4: U '#/kilo
A5: U 'Air Freight :
C5: U 1.21
D5: U '#/kilo
A7: U 'Item
B7: U 'Weight/kg
C7: U 'Price - $
D7: U 'Price - #
E7: U 'Cost - #
F7: U 'Cost - #

E8: U 'Sea
F8: U 'Air
A9: U 'AD016
B9: U 40
C9: U 67
D9: U +C9/C3
E9: U +B9*C4+D9
F9: U +B9*C5+D9
A10: U 'AD017
B10: U 23
C10: U 55
D10: U +C10/C3
E10: U +B10*C4+D10
F10: U +B10*C5+D10
A11: U 'AD018
B11: U 12

Fig 2.20 *Contents of freight costs sheet (continued)*

C15: U 340
D15: U +C15/C3
E15: U +B15*C4+D15
F15: U +B15*C5+D15
A16: U 'JT068
B16: U 122
C16: U 400
D16: U +C16/C3
E16: U +B16*C4+D16
F16: U +B16*C5+D16
A17: U 'JT070
B17: U 160
C17: U 450
D17: U +C17/C3
E17: U +B17*C4+D17
F17: U +B17*C5+D17
A18: U 'JT098
B18: U 180
C18: U 500
D18: U +C18/C3
E18: U +B18*C4+D18
F18: U +B18*C5+D18
C11: U 34

D11: U +C11/C3
E11: U +B11*C4+D11
F11: U +B11*C5+D11
A12: U 'PD089
B12: U 45
C12: U 78
D12: U +C12/C3
E12: U +B12*C4+D12
F12: U +B12*C5+D12
A13: U 'PD090
B13: U 43
C13: U 89
D13: U +C13/C3
E13: U +B13*C4+D13
F13: U +B13*C5+D13
A14: U 'PD099
B14: U 31
C14: U 90
D14: U +C14/C3
E14: U +B14*C4+D14
F14: U +B14*C5+D14
A15: U 'JT067
B15: U 100

SUMMARY

1. A spreadsheet program provides you with the electronic equivalent of a very large sheet of paper divided into "cells" each referenced by its row and column identifiers.
2. Text (i.e. words), data (i.e. numbers) or formulas can be entered in any cell.
3. A formula tells the program what operations to perform on the entries in one or more cells.
4. Once a spreadsheet has been created it can be saved on disk for future use and it can be printed out to be incorporated in a report if required.
5. The entries in all the cells, text, data and formulas, can be printed out in order for you to see how a spreadsheet is constructed.
6. Once a spreadsheet has been created a change in any one of the entries can cause the entire sheet to be recalculated. This enables you to play the "what if I" game.

COMING TO TERMS

This chapter explains and illustrates a number of the features common to most of the spreadsheet programs on the market at the time of writing.

3.1 FORMULAS

Every spreadsheet needs to have the ability to perform the normal arithmetic operations of adding, subtracting, multiplying, dividing and raising a number to a power. In addition it needs to recognise the meaning of left-hand and right-hand brackets embedded in a formula. The evaluation of formulas will generally follow the accepted rules of arithmetic, but check that this is so with the spreadsheet you are using. The order of evaluation will be that anything enclosed inside brackets is dealt with first of all. Then any calculations that involve raising a number to a power are performed. Then any multiplication and division and finally any addition and subtraction. When nothing but operations of equal status are carried out they are carried out from left to right. For example the stages in working out the expression

$$2 + (3\wedge2 * 4) - (4*3 - 3)*2$$

are:

1. $2 + (9 * 4) - (12 - 3)*2$
2. $2 + 36 - 9*2$
3. $2 + 36 - 18$
4. $2 + 18$
5. 20

It is advisable to check the order of calculation of your spreadsheet formulas since if you have one that evaluates from left to right without worrying about precedence except for brackets you could get

1.   2 + (9 * 4) - (12 - 3)*2
2.   2 + 36 - 9*2
3.   29*2
4.   58

which is not what is intended.

All spreadsheets provide a wide range of "built in" formulas, called "functions", that cut down a lot of work for the user. You have already seen the use of the **sum** function. But there are many more. Whatever spreadsheet you use the functions tend to have the same, or certainly very similar, names. Here is a list of the commonest used in arithmetic calculations:

Function	Use
Sum	Totals the cells listed
Average	Calculates the average of the numbers listed
Count	Counts the number of non-zero numbers listed
Max	Displays the largest number in the list
Min	Displays the smallest number in the list
Var	Displays the variance of the numbers in the list
Stdev	Calculates the standard deviation of the list
Rand	Displays a random number in the range 0 to 1
Round	Rounds a number to a specified number of places
Sqrt	Calculates the square root of a number
Int	Displays the whole number part of a number
Pi	Displays 3.1415926 . . . .

Many standard functions are available for mathematicians to use: sine, cosine, tangent, arc sine, arc cosine and arc tangent together with exponential functions and logarithms. For financial calculations there are functions to calculate future values, present values, interest rates, periodic payments to pay off a principal and internal rates of return, to mention just few. The worksheet shown in Figure 3.1 shows a few of the arithmetic functions in use. Figure 3.2 shows the list of the contents of the cells. You should notice the way in which the functions are used; A3 . . H3 means "all the cells in the range from A3 to H3". The contents of the brackets are referred to as the "argument".

A particularly useful function to have, and it is in all spreadsheet programs, is the one that makes the program take decisions. The keyword that is used is **IF**. It works in the following way; if you had a situation where, for example, discount was allowed if the amount of the bill exceeded 50 pounds. In that case 5% discount was allowed. For all bills under that value no discount was given. The layout of a formula that uses the **IF** function is always of the form

IF(test,answer if test is true, answer if test is false)

In Figure 3.3 you will see that there are two examples in one. The first calculates discount of 5% if the order is over 50 pounds. The second allows a more complicated discount structure giving 10% for bills over 100 pounds, 5% for those over 50 pounds and nothing for bills below 50 pounds. When the contents of the cells are listed out, as shown in Figure 3.4 you will see that cell D3 contains the formula

IF(D2>50,D2*.05,0)

which is the spreadsheet's way of saying "If the number in cell D2 exceeds 50 then multiply the contents of that cell by 0.05 and display the answer. If the contents of D2 equal 50 or are less than 50 then display zero". In the second example the formula in D9 contains one "IF" nested inside another:

IF(D8>100,D8*.1,IF(D8>50,D8*.05,0))

Fig 3.1 *Examples of functions*

```
A1: U 'Examples of spreadsheet functions                          READY

        A         B         C         D       E       F       G       H
 1  Examples of spreadsheet functions
 2
 3      12.3     14.4      12.3     10.7     12.6   18.9      3     5.9
 4
 5      90.1 Sum
 6    11.2625 Average
 7   3.355964 Square root
 8      18.9 Maximum
 9         3 Minimum
10        62 Sum of odd entries
11   3.141592 3.141592
12         8 Number of entries
13
14
15
16
17
18
19
20
25-Nov-88   12:13 AM
```

Fig 3.2 *List of spreadsheet contents*

A1: U 'Examples of spreadsheet functions

A3: U 12.3

B3: U 14.4

C3: U 12.3

D3: U 10.7

E3: U 12.6

F3: U 18.9

G3: U 3

H3: U 5.9

A5: U @SUM(A3..H3)

B5: U 'Sum

A6: U @AVG(A3..H3)

B6: U 'Average

A7: U @SQRT(A6)

B7: U 'Square root

A8: U @MAX(A3..H3)

B8: U 'Maximum

A9: U @MIN(A3..H3)

B9: U 'Minimum

A10: U @SUM(A3,C3,E3,F3,H3)

B10: U 'Sum of odd entries

A11: U @PI

B11: U @PI

A12: U @COUNT(A3..H3)

B12: U 'Number of entries

46

Fig 3.3 *Using IF*

```
F12:                                                    READY

      A       B        C        D      E      F        G        H
1
2             Amount of bill     56.78
3             Discount            2.84         5% discount on orders
4             Total:             53.94         over £50
5
6
7
8             Amount of bill    102.55         10% discount on orders
9             Discount           10.26         over £100, 5% on
10            Total:             92.30         orders over £50
11
12
13
14
15
16
17
18
19
20
25-Nov-88  12:15 AM
```

Fig 3.4 *List of contents of discount sheet*

B2: U 'Amount of bill
D2: (F2) U 56.78
B3: U 'Discount
D3: (F2) U @IF(D2>50,D2*0.05,0)
F3: U '5% discount on orders
B4: U 'Total:
D4: (F2) U +D2-D3
F4: U 'over #50
B8: U 'Amount of bill
D8: (F2) U 102.55
F8: U '10% discount on orders
B9: U 'Discount
D9: (F2) U @IF(D8>100,D8*0.1,@IF(D8>50,D8*0.05,0))
F9: U 'over #100, 5% on
B10: U 'Total:
D10: (F2) U +D8-D9
F10: U 'orders over #50

which says "If the contents of D8 exceed 100 then multiply the contents of that cell by 0.1 and display the answer. If the contents of D8 are equal to or less than 100 then test them again and if the contents exceed 50 then multiply by 0.05 and display. Otherwise display zero".

The point of the nested test above is that if the bill is not greater than 100 pounds then it can still lie between 50 and 100 pounds, hence the same test as is shown in the first part of the example is used.

IFs can be nested as much as you wish but then can become very complex. An alternative way of doing this will be shown in section 3.6.

3.2 FORMATTING

So far you will have noticed that although the spread-sheet is doing a good job of calculating it does not appear to be very good at displaying the information in an attractive manner. For example, the amounts of money do not really look like amounts of money as they are often displayed to more than two places of decimals. Also, the text is very often squashed up against the wrong edge of a column. These problems can all be dealt with by using the technique of "formatting" the display. This allows the display to be much easier to read and lets you lay it out in a more meaningful manner. Spreadsheet programs give you a very wide range of options for the display of information.

Most spreadsheets, if left to their own devices, will display a number in such a way as to put as much information as possible into a cell. This means that as many decimal places will be shown as can be put into the available space and if this cannot be done then a number will be displayed in scientific format. Scientific format is of particular use in displaying very large or very small numbers by writing them down as

3.456E10

instead of

34560000000

The E in fact stands for "times ten to the power of" since 34560000000 is the same as 3.456 x 10 x 10 x 10 x 10 x 10 x 10 x 10 x 10 x 10 x 10.

The usual choices given to you for formatting numerical entries are as follows:

Integer	To nearest whole number
Scientific	In the form X.XXEXX
Currency	In the form X,XXX.XX (Currency format often places negative amounts in brackets as well)
Percent	Multiplies the number by 100 and places a % sign after it.
Fixed	Displays a number to a specified number of decimal places usually between 0 and 15
+	Converts the number to nearest whole number and displays that number of + signs. Used for displaying simple graphs

Text entries can often be displayed ranged to the right of their column, ranged to the left or centered in the column. In addition, column widths can be changed and in some cases brought down to zero width.

Another way that you can see the contents of cells consisting of formulas is to turn the entry into a text entry. This is quicker to use than the method used to produce the listings shown already. The only problem raised by doing this is that if a formula has more characters in it that the width of the cell then the right-hand part of the formula is truncated. Figure 3.5 shows the worksheet displayed in Figure 2.19 but properly formatted. You should notice how the widths of the cells have been changed in order to make the sheet look better. When printed out, as shown in Figure 3.6, it is much neater and tidier than it was before.

Figure 3.7 shows the same sheet displaying the contents of the formula cells. As you can see, the full contents of a cell can be displayed on the entry line when the cursor is on that cell.

Fig 3.5 *Formatted sheet*

```
A1: U [W6] 'Glendale Hardware Ltd                                    READY

        A           B          C           D          E         F
 1   Glendale Hardware Ltd
 2
 3   Rate of exchange:        1.56          $/£
 4   Sea Freight :            0.54          £/kilo
 5   Air Freight :            1.21          £/kilo
 6
 7   Item        Weight/kg   Price - $   Price - £   Cost - £   Cost - £
 8                                                     Sea        Air
 9   ----------------------------------------------------------------------
10   AD016            40      67.00       42.95      64.55      91.35
11   AD017            23      55.00       35.26      47.68      63.09
12   AD018            12      34.00       21.79      28.27      36.31
13   PD089            45      78.00       50.00      74.30     104.45
14   PD090            43      89.00       57.05      80.27     109.08
15   PD099            31      90.00       57.69      74.43      95.20
16   JT067           100     340.00      217.95     271.95     338.95
17   JT068           122     400.00      256.41     322.29     404.03
18   JT070           160     450.00      288.46     374.86     482.06
19   JT098           180     500.00      320.51     417.71     538.31
20
25-Nov-88   12:17 AM
```

Fig 3.6 *Printout of formatted sheet*

```
Glendale Hardware Ltd

Rate of exchange:        1.56          $/£
Sea Freight :            0.54          £/kilo
Air Freight :            1.21          £/kilo

Item        Weight/kg   Price - $   Price - £   Cost - £   Cost - £
                                                  Sea        Air
----------------------------------------------------------------------
AD016            40      67.00       42.95      64.55      91.35
AD017            23      55.00       35.26      47.68      63.09
AD018            12      34.00       21.79      28.27      36.31
PD089            45      78.00       50.00      74.30     104.45
PD090            43      89.00       57.05      80.27     109.08
PD099            31      90.00       57.69      74.43      95.20
JT067           100     340.00      217.95     271.95     338.95
JT068           122     400.00      256.41     322.29     404.03
JT070           160     450.00      288.46     374.86     482.06
JT098           180     500.00      320.51     417.71     538.31
```

50

Fig 3.7 *Contents of formatted sheet*

```
E10:  (T) U [W12] +B10*C4+D10                                        READY

        A        B           C           D        E           F
1    Glendale Hardware Ltd
2
3    Rate of exchange:        1.56        $/£
4    Sea Freight :            0.54        £/kilo
5    Air Freight :            1.21        £/kilo
6
7    Item    Weight/kg    Price - $    Price - £   Cost - £    Cost - £
8                                                  Sea         Air
9    -----------------------------------------------------------------
10   ADO16       40         67.00        42.95   +B10*C4+D10 +B10*C5+D10
11   ADO17       23         55.00        35.26   +B11*C4+D11 +B11*C5+D11
12   ADO18       12         34.00        21.79   +B12*C4+D12 +B12*C5+D12
13   PDO89       45         78.00        50.00   +B13*C4+D13 +B13*C5+D13
14   PDO90       43         89.00        57.05   +B14*C4+D14 +B14*C5+D14
15   PDO99       31         90.00        57.69   +B15*C4+D15 +B15*C5+D15
16   JTO67      100        340.00       217.95   +B16*C4+D16 +B16*C5+D16
17   JTO68      122        400.00       256.41   +B17*C4+D17 +B17*C5+D17
18   JTO70      160        450.00       288.46   +B18*C4+D18 +B18*C5+D18
19   JTO98      180        500.00       320.51   +B19*C4+D19 +B19*C5+D19
20
25-Nov-88  12:02 AM
```

The output from the last example, Figures 3.5, 3.6, 3.7, has been enhanced by having a line of dashes drawn across the page. All the spreadsheets have the facility for repeating characters across the page in order to improve the legibility of the output.

3.3 INSERTING NEW ROWS AND COLUMNS

In order to create a row whereby you can draw the line across the screen there is a very useful spreadsheet feature that enables you to move sections of the sheet down or to the right and insert one or more extra rows or columns. The columns that have been moved to make way for the insertions have any cell references amended to take account of their new positions. You can notice this in the example shown in Figure 3.7. Compare it with the listing shown in Figure 2.20. All the entries on row 9 have been moved to row 10 and so on down the sheet so that the new row 19 has the formula that was in row 18 but with the references correctly adjusted.

3.4 PROTECTING AND HIDING CELLS

Very often when you create a worksheet you will have spent a lot of time and patience getting the formulas right. What you do not want to happen is that by accident data in entered into the wrong cell, one that already contains a formula for example. Most spreadsheet programs allow you to protect certain key cells from being overwritten so that even if you try in error to enter a piece of data into the wrong cell the computer will "beep" at you and display a message to tell you that this cannot be done. This will certainly save you from a lot of heartache.

The example shown in Figure 3.8 shows a worksheet that has had certain key cells protected. The object of the sheet should be self-evident as it allows you to calculate the net profit or loss in a small coffee bar (it only sells buns and coffee!). The layout of the screen is shown in Figure 3.8 but when you see the listing of the contents of the cells, shown in Figure 3.9, you will see that the cells that are protected are identified by a **P**. You should notice that, in fact it is only the cells in the ranges B4:B9 and B13:B16 and cell B18 that are unprotected.

Fig 3.8 *Coffee bar worksheet*

	A || B || C || D
1	Break Even Example		Cups Sold	Buns sold
2	--			
3			100	125
4	Coffee per cup	.35	200	125
5	Price per bun	.25	300	125
6	No. of buns sold	125	400	125
7	Rent	50.00	500	125
8	Wages	100.00	600	125
9	Electricity	20.00	700	125
10	TOTAL weekly cost	170.00	800	125
11			900	125
12	Cost per cup		1000	125
13	Coffee	.03	1100	125
14	Milk	.01	1200	125
15	Breakages	.05	1300	125
16	Sugar	.02	1400	125
17	TOTAL cost per cup	.11	1500	125
18	Cost of Buns	.10	1600	125
19	Quantity Increment	100	1700	125
20			1800	125

Fig 3.9 *Contents of protected sheet*

A1		P= " Break Even Example
C1	TR	P= "Cups Sold
D1	GTR	P= "Buns sold
E1		P= "Profit or Loss
A2		P= '-
C3		P= B19
D3		P= B6
E3		P= C3*B4+B6*(B5-B18)-(B10+(B17*C3))
A4		P= "Coffee per cup
B4		= .35

E30	P= C30*B4+B6*(B5-B18)-(B10+(B17*C30))
C31	P= C30+B19
D31	P= B6
E31	P= C31*B4+B6*(B5-B18)-(B10+(B17*C31))
C32	P= C31+B19
D32	P= B6
E32	P= C32*B4+B6*(B5-B18)-(B10+(B17*C32))
C33	P= C32+B19
D33	P= B6
E33	P= C33*B4+B6*(B5-B18)-(B10+(B17*C33))

3.5 COPYING AND MOVING

All spreadsheets have the facility to allow you to copy
the contents of one or more cells into a specified range
of empty cells. This enables you to produce a complicated formula and then reproduce it as many times as you
wish without the tedium of having to enter it over and
over again. The spreadsheet programs will all modify the
cell references as the copying proceeds. In addition it
is always possible to suppress this modification if
required. A term used in some spreadsheets is "Replicating" rather than "Copying", although SuperCalc uses
both!

The form of a copying instruction is to specify the
cell or range of cells to be copied and then specify the
"target" range. The type of copying that generally can
be done is:

    1. Copy the contents of one cell into another cell
    2. Copy the contents of one cell into a range of
       cells; part of a row, part of a column or a block

3. Copy a partial row or column into another partial row or column

The important thing to remember when copying, or replicating, is that you have to specify the range you are copying but you do not always have to specify the range into which the copy is placed. For example, if you wish to copy the contents of one cell into a range of cells then obviously that target range must be specified exactly. If however you are going to copy a range of cells into another range of the same size then all you need to do is to specify the top left-hand cell of that range and the program will do the rest for you. Some examples of this taking place are shown in Figures 3.10 to 3.18.

In Figure 3.10 there are two entries only, in cells A1 and A2, on a Lotus 1-2-3 worksheet. A1 contains the figure 100 and A2 contains the formula +A1+10. First of all the formula in A2 is to be copied into the partial column A3:A20 and the screens shown in Figures 3.11 and 3.12 display the sequence of commands. The final result is shown in Figure 3.13. Then the entire column is copied into the partial column B1:B20 using the commands as shown in Figures 3.14 and 3.15. The final result is shown in Figure 3.16. You should notice that the formula has been adjusted automatically from the display in cell B10.

The sheet shown in Figure 3.17 has a block of four entries that are going to be copied into another block on the sheet. Notice that in Figure 3.18 the target range is specified only by its top left-hand corner. The result is shown in Figure 3.19.

Cells, or blocks of cells, can be moved rather than copied. The actual effect of this is a copying operation followed by a deletion of the original block. Figures 3.20 and 3.21 show the block D4:E5 about to be moved to a block with its top left-hand corner in cell A7. The final result is displayed in Figure 3.22. Note again that cell references are adjusted just as with replication.

54

Fig 3.10 *First part of copy command*

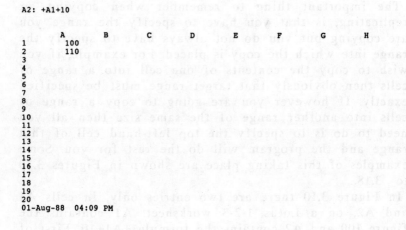

```
A2: +A1+10

        A      B      C      D      E      F      G      H
 1     100
 2     110
 3
 4
 5
 6
 7
 8
 9
10
11
12
13
14
15
16
17
18
19
20
01-Aug-88   04:09 PM
```

Fig 3.11 *First part of sheet to be copied*

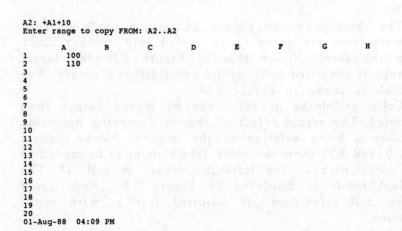

```
A2: +A1+10
Enter range to copy FROM: A2..A2

        A      B      C      D      E      F      G      H
 1     100
 2     110
 3
 4
 5
 6
 7
 8
 9
10
11
12
13
14
15
16
17
18
19
20
01-Aug-88   04:09 PM
```

Fig 3.12 *Second part of copy command*

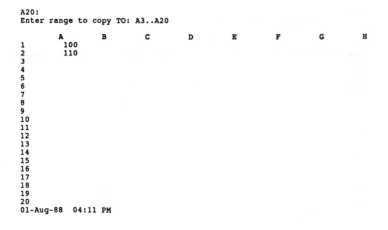

```
A20:
Enter range to copy TO: A3..A20

        A       B       C       D       E       F       G       H
1      100
2      110
3
4
5
6
7
8
9
10
11
12
13
14
15
16
17
18
19
20
01-Aug-88   04:11 PM
```

Fig 3.13 *Copying complete*

```
A2: +A1+10

        A       B       C       D       E       F       G       H
1      100
2      110
3      120
4      130
5      140
6      150
7      160
8      170
9      180
10     190
11     200
12     210
13     220
14     230
15     240
16     250
17     260
18     270
19     280
20     290
01-Aug-88   04:12 PM
```

Fig 3.14 *Column to be copied*

```
A20: +A19+10
Enter range to copy FROM: A1..A20

          A       B       C       D       E       F       G       H
1         100
2         110
3         120
4         130
5         140
6         150
7         160
8         170
9         180
10        190
11        200
12        210
13        220
14        230
15        240
16        250
17        260
18        270
19        280
20        290
01-Aug-88  04:12 PM
```

Fig 3.15 *Target for copying identified*

```
B1:
Enter range to copy TO: B1

          A       B       C       D       E       F       G       H
1         100
2         110
3         120
4         130
5         140
6         150
7         160
8         170
9         180
10        190
11        200
12        210
13        220
14        230
15        240
16        250
17        260
18        270
19        280
20        290
01-Aug-88  04:13 PM
```

Fig 3.16 *Copying complete*

B2: +B1+10

```
        A         B         C         D         E         F         G         H
1      100       100
2      110       110
3      120       120
4      130       130
5      140       140
6      150       150
7      160       160
8      170       170
9      180       180
10     190       190
11     200       200
12     210       210
13     220       220
14     230       230
15     240       240
16     250       250
17     260       260
18     270       270
19     280       280
20     290       290
01-Aug-88   04:14 PM
```

Fig 3.17 *Copying a block*

A1: 100

```
        A         B         C         D         E         F         G         H
1      100       100
2      110       110
3
4
5
6
7
8
9
10
11
12
13
14
15
16
17
18
19
20
01-Aug-88   04:15 PM
```

58

Fig 3.18 *Target for copied block*

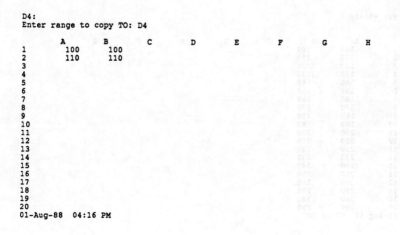

```
D4:
Enter range to copy TO: D4

        A        B        C        D        E        F        G        H
1      100      100
2      110      110
3
4
5
6
7
8
9
10
11
12
13
14
15
16
17
18
19
20
01-Aug-88   04:16 PM
```

Fig 3.19 *Copying complete*

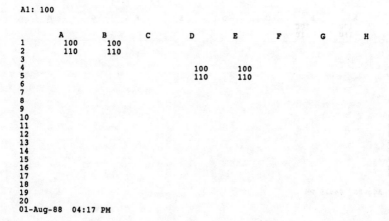

```
A1: 100

        A        B        C        D        E        F        G        H
1      100      100
2      110      110
3
4                                100      100
5                                110      110
6
7
8
9
10
11
12
13
14
15
16
17
18
19
20
01-Aug-88   04:17 PM
```

Fig 3.20 *Range for move defined*

```
E5: +E4+10
Enter range to move FROM: D4..E5

          A         B         C         D         E         F         G         H
1        100       100
2        110       110
3
4                                      100       100
5                                      110       110
6
7
8
9
10
11
12
13
14
15
16
17
18
19
20
01-Aug-88   04:22 PM
```

Fig 3.21 *Target for move defined*

```
A7:
Enter range to move TO: A7

          A         B         C         D         E         F         G         H
1        100       100
2        110       110
3
4                                      100       100
5                                      110       110
6
7
8
9
10
11
12
13
14
15
16
17
18
19
20
01-Aug-88   04:23 PM
```

60

Fig 3.22 *Move complete*

```
D4:

      A         B         C      D      E      F      G      H
1       100       100
2       110       110
3
4
5
6
7       100       100
8       110       110
9
10
11
12
13
14
15
16
17
18
19
20
01-Aug-88  04:23 PM
```

3.6 TABLE LOOKUP

In an earlier example in section 3.1 you saw how different rates of discount can be applied, but if a large range of discounts were offered this would lead to producing some horrific formulas. However, you can incorporate these in a table that can be accessed by the spreadsheet program. The next example shows how this can be used. First of all in Figure 3.23 you can see a worksheet that calculates the amount of discount given on amounts spent in different bands. The sheet has been created in this instance by the Quattro spreadsheet program. The cursor has been placed in cell C7 and you can see that a quite complicated set of IF formulas are used. A much better way to do the same thing is shown in the next example shown in Figure 3.24 where the entries in column C have been replaced with references to a "lookup" table. The actual contents of the sheet are shown in this example and the table used is held in the block A16:B19. The entries down the left-hand side represent the bands eligible for discount and the numbers beside each entry are the rates of discount. The formula

LOOKUP(A7,A16:B19)

in cell C7 is saying "Find the entry corresponding to the contents of cell A7 in the partial column A16:B19. Return the number beside the appropriate entry". The table works so that if the number 1000 or less is found in the table then a discount of zero is applied. If the number lies in the range 1001 to 1500 then a discount of 0.05 (5%) is applied and so on. This is not exactly the way a lookup table works on every spreadsheet, but they are all very similar to one another. A discount table is easy to amend whereas if the discounts change and the IF statement version is used then there is a lot of complicated editing to do before a new discount structure can be used. The table can be hidden if this feature is available on the spreadsheet program you are using. Some spreadsheets will only do it by reducing the width of a complete column to zero, which would mean resiting the discount table to the right of the main part of the worksheet.

Fig 3.23 *A series of IFs used in sheet*

```
     A         B          C          D        E        F         G        H
 1   20% discount given for order's over £2000
 2   10% discount given for orders over £1500
 3   5% discount given for orders over £1000
 4   ==================================================================
 5   Amount    Date       % Discount Discount Net      VAT       Total
 6   ------------------------------------------------------------------
 7   1,510.00  12/03/88        0.1    151.00 1,359.00   203.85 1,562.85
 8   1,200.00  14/09/88        0.05    60.00 1,140.00   171.00 1,311.00
 9   1,450.00  12/11/88        0.05    72.50 1,377.50   206.63 1,584.13
10     340.00  09/04/88        0       0.00   340.00    51.00   391.00
11   2,341.00  05/02/88        0.2    468.20 1,872.80   280.92 2,153.72
12   3,000.00  23/12/88        0.2    600.00 2,400.00   360.00 2,760.00
13   5,020.00  01/05/88        0.2  1,004.00 4,016.00   602.40 4,618.40
14     100.00  03/10/88        0       0.00   100.00    15.00   115.00
15
16
17
18
19
20
C7:  [W11] @IF(A7>2000,0.2,@IF(A7>1500,0.1,(@IF(A7>1000,
25-Nov-88   12:28 AM                                         READY
```

Fig 3.24 *Contents of sheet using a lookup table*

```
         A        B        C         D       E        F        G        H
 1   20% discount given for orders over £2000
 2   10% discount given for orders over £1500
 3   5% discount given for orders over £1000
 4   ================================================================
 5   Amount    Date      % Discount Discount Net      VAT      Total
 6   ----------------------------------------------------------------
 7   1,510.00 12/03/88      0.1     151.00 1,359.00  203.85 1,562.85
 8   1,200.00 14/09/88      0.05     60.00 1,140.00  171.00 1,311.00
 9   1,450.00 12/11/88      0.05     72.50 1,377.50  206.63 1,584.13
10     340.00 09/04/88      0         0.00   340.00   51.00   391.00
11   2,341.00 05/02/88      0.2     468.20 1,872.80  280.92 2,153.72
12   3,000.00 23/12/88      0.2     600.00 2,400.00  360.00 2,760.00
13   5,020.00 01/05/88      0.2   1,004.00 4,016.00  602.40 4,618.40
14     100.00 03/10/88      0         0.00   100.00   15.00   115.00
15
16           0           0
17        1000        0.05
18        1500        0.1
19        2000        0.2
20
C7:  [W11] @VLOOKUP(A7,$A$16..$B$19,1)
25-Nov-88  12:26 AM                                              READY
```

3.7 TITLES

Very often if you have a large spreadsheet that extends beyond the size of your display on the screen you could find yourself in the position of seeing numbers and entries that were difficult to identify as they are now a long way from the title of the column or row they are associated with. It is possible therefore to hold the titles firm on the screen so that wherever you may be they are still displayed.

The example shown in Figure 3.25 has been created in Perfect Calc II. You will see that it is the same worksheet as was shown in Figures 3.23 and 3.24, but with extra entries. You should notice that the **LOOKUP** function is being used again but the table has had to be changed since the function works slightly differently on this program, as you were warned in the previous section. In this case it is saying "If the number is greater than zero and less than 1001 then the discount is zero. If the number is greater than 1001 but less

than 1501 then the discount is 0.05 (5%)", and so on.
Because there are more rows in the spreadsheet it is
useful to have the titles retained at the top of the
sheet. There is usually some sort of **TITLES** command to
do this for you so that the screen above the cursor
position when the command was given is "frozen". This
enables you to progress down the sheet with extra
entries while the titles remain. The effect is shown in
Figure 3.25. The whole spreadsheet as printed out is
shown in Figure 3.26.

Fig 3.25 *Title held at top of screen*

```
   |   a   |   b   |   c   |   d   |   e   |   f   |
   120% discount given for orders over 2000
   210% discount given for orders over 1500
   35% discount given for orders over 1000
   4===========================================================
   5Amount Date      % Discount  Discount    Net        VAT
   6-----------------------------------------------------------
   201640.0012/12/87      0.10    164.00    1476.00    221.40
   21 190.0001/02/87         0         0     190.00     28.50
   228900.0031/01/87      0.20   1780.00    7120.00   1068.00
   237800.0001/04/87      0.20   1560.00    6240.00    936.00
   246700.0023/07/87      0.20   1340.00    5360.00    804.00
   25
   26      0          0
   271001.00       0.05
   281501.00       0.10
   292001.00       0.20
   30
   31
   32
   33
   34
   35
   36
                                          B:DISCOUNT.PC a36
```

Fig 3.26 *Printout of complete sheet*

```
20% discount given for orders over #2000
10% discount given for orders over #1500
5% discount given for orders over #1000
========================================================================
Amount Date      % Discount  Discount    Net        VAT       Total
------------------------------------------------------------------------
1510.0012/03/87      0.10    151.00    1359.00    203.85    1562.
1200.0011/02/87      0.05     60.00    1140.00    171.00    1311.
1450.0013/01/87      0.05     72.50    1377.50    206.63    1584.
 340.0015/12/87         0        0      340.00     51.00     391.
2341.0031/12/86      0.20    468.20    1872.80    280.92    2153.
3000.0009/01/87      0.20    600.00    2400.00    360.00    2760.
5020.0014/01/87      0.20   1004.00    4016.00    602.40    4618.
 100.0021/02/87         0        0      100.00     15.00     115.
 201.0019/07/87         0        0      201.00     30.15     231.
1389.0017/06/87      0.05     69.45    1319.55    197.93    1517.
2005.0008/08/87      0.20    401.00    1604.00    240.60    1844.
 123.0001/01/87         0        0      123.00     18.45     141.
  10.0014/03/87         0        0       10.00      1.50      11.
1640.0012/12/87      0.10    164.00    1476.00    221.40    1697.
 190.0001/02/87         0        0      190.00     28.50     218.
8900.0031/01/87      0.20   1780.00    7120.00   1068.00    8188.
7800.0001/04/87      0.20   1560.00    6240.00    936.00    7176.
6700.0023/07/87      0.20   1340.00    5360.00    804.00    6164.

   0          0
1001.00       0.05
1501.00       0.10
2001.00       0.20
```

3.8 WINDOWS

Another feature of spreadsheet programs that makes it easier to use large worksheets is the "windowing" feature. By using this it is possible to see two parts of the sheet at the same time on the screen. It is easy to move from one of these "windows" on the sheet to the other, scroll through the data on one window only or synchronise the scrolling of both windows. A worksheet can be split vertically or horizontally into windows. Examples are shown in Figures 3.27 and 3.28.

Fig 3.27 *Effect of a vertical window*

```
   |  a  |   b     | |  |   e    |   f    |   g     |  h   |
   120% discount given   1
   210% discount given   2
   35% discount given f  3
   4==================   4=================================================
   5Amount Date          5Net          VAT          Total
   6------------------   6--------------------------------------------------
   71510.0012/03/87      7     1359.00      203.85      1562.85
   81200.0011/02/87      8     1140.00      171.00      1311.00
   91450.0013/01/87      9     1377.50      206.63      1584.13
   10 340.0015/12/87     10     340.00       51.00       391.00
   112341.0031/12/86     11    1872.80      280.92      2153.72
   123000.0009/01/87     12    2400.00      360.00      2760.00
   135020.0014/01/87     13    4016.00      602.40      4618.40
   14 100.0021/02/87     14     100.00       15.00       115.00
   15 201.0019/07/87     15     201.00       30.15       231.15
   161389.0017/06/87     16    1319.55      197.93      1517.48
   172005.0008/08/87     17    1604.00      240.60      1844.60
   18 123.0001/01/87     18     123.00       18.45       141.45
   19  10.0014/03/87     19      10.00        1.50        11.50
   201640.0012/12/87     20    1476.00      221.40      1697.40
   21 190.0001/02/87     21     190.00       28.50       218.50
   228900.0031/01/87     22    7120.00     1068.00      8188.00
   237800.0001/04/87     23    6240.00      936.00      7176.00
                                                  B:DISCOUNT.PC h5
```

Fig 3.28 *Effect of a horizontal window*

```
   |  a  |   b    |   c    |   d    |   e    |   f   |
   120% discount given for orders over #2000
   210% discount given for orders over #1500
   35% discount given for orders over #1000
   4==========================================================
   5Amount Date      % Discount  Discount    Net          VAT
   6-------------------------------------------------------------
   |  a  |   b    |   c    |   d    |   e    |   f   |
   15 201.0019/07/87           0         0     201.00       30.15
   161389.0017/06/87        0.05     69.45    1319.55      197.93
   172005.0008/08/87        0.20    401.00    1604.00      240.60
   18 123.0001/01/87           0         0     123.00       18.45
   19  10.0014/03/87           0         0      10.00        1.50
   201640.0012/12/87        0.10    164.00    1476.00      221.40
   21 190.0001/02/87           0         0     190.00       28.50
   228900.0031/01/87        0.20   1780.00    7120.00     1068.00
   237800.0001/04/87        0.20   1560.00    6240.00      936.00
   246700.0023/07/87        0.20   1340.00    5360.00      804.00
   25
   26    0           0
   271001.00         0.05
   281501.00         0.10
   292001.00         0.20
   30
                                            B:DISCOUNT.PC a30
```

3.9 RECALCULATION

On a small spreadsheet it takes very little time to recalculate the value of every cell as a new piece of data is added. However, on a large sheet, possibly with some heavy calculation to do, this can take an appreciable time. Automatic recalculation can be switched off therefore and this allows you to enter your data quickly without having to wait several seconds while the program goes off and does its arithmetic. When you want recalculation finally to take place you usually have to press the ! key and the whole sheet will change to give the final new display.

The order in which calculations take place is also capable of being modified. Recalculation can take place in three different ways:

1. In "natural" order, where cells containing a reference to another cell have those cells evaluated before the cell itself can be evaluated

2. Row by row from top to bottom where each row is evaluated from left to right first

3. Column by column from left to right where each column is evaluated from top to bottom first

In general it is safest to have all cells that contain references to other cells to be below and to the right of those cells. If you do not you will have what are called "forward" or "backward" references and the result of having them is that you may have to recalculate twice in order to obtain the correct display. The normal, or default, setting of most spreadsheets is to perform calculations in natural order.

3.10 CIRCULAR REFERENCES

There are times when either by accident or design you have a cell that either directly or by implication refers to itself. For example, in cell D4 you may have the formula D4+1. A more complex one is where one cell refers to another cell, it to another cell still and finally that cell refers back to the original. This will usually be picked up by the program to tell you that you have a "circular" reference. There are occasions where this is of value, in some mathematical worksheets where the process of iteration takes place. These are described later on (p.126). At other times such references are a source of problems and have to be eliminated. It can be quite a task looking for circular references. A program such as Lotus HAL enables you to indulge in the auditing of Lotus 1-2-3 worksheets to find out what cells depend on each other. Using this can help you to seek out circular references.

3.11 LOGICAL EXPRESSIONS

You have already seen that you can arrange for your spreadsheet program to make logical decisions that are in fact based on the truth or otherwise of a statement, **B4>1500** for example. If this is TRUE then one thing happens if it is FALSE then another thing happens. The use of truth values can be extended by using the logical expressions **AND, OR**, and **NOT**. Examples of the use of the first two of these are shown in Figures 3.29 and 3.30. The first example, in the range A1:C5, has the answers to the questions entered in C1, C2 and C3. The key instruction is in A5 where an IF instruction is combined with AND and OR. It is the spreadsheet's way of saying "If the entry in C1 AND either the entry in C2 or C3 are both "Yes" then the first phrase is displayed. Otherwise the second phrase is displayed". In the second example, in the range A8:C12, there are three questions and hence three answers. In this case what the instruction is saying is that "If the entry in C8 is "Yes" and C9 contains "Yes" and C10 does not contain "Yes" then the first phrase is displayed, otherwise the second phrase is displayed".

The use of **NOT** reverses what is called the "Truth Value" of a statement. This is because if a statement is TRUE then it is evaluated by the program to be unity (the number 1). A statement that is FALSE is evaluated to zero. Similarly zero equates to FALSE and any other number (that is, any number that is not zero) equates to TRUE. It thus becomes quite easy to see that **NOT(an expression)** reverses its truth value so that non-zero numbers become zero and zeros become 1's. Anyone who has studied some mathematics will have met truth tables that define the actual meanings of logical AND and OR.

Fig 3.29 *Use of logical expressions*

	A	B	C
1	Weather good ?		Yes
2	Is my car ready ?		No
3	Is your car ready ?		No
4			
5	Let's stay at home		
6			
7			
8	Weather good ?		Yes
9	Can I have the car ?		Yes
10	Is the petrol tank empty ?		No
11			
12	Let's go for a picnic		
13			

Fig 3.30 *Contents of logical spreadsheet*

	A	B	C
1	"Weather good ?	"Yes	
2	"is my car ready ?	"No	
3	"is your car ready ?	"No	
4	+IF(AND(c1="Yes",OR(c2="Yes",c3="Yes")),"Let's go for a picnic","Let's stay at home")		
5			
6	"Weather good ?	"Yes	
8	"Can I have the car ?	"Yes	
9	"Is the petrol tank empty ?	"No	
10			
11	+IF(AND((c8="Yes"),AND(c9="Yes",NOT(c10="Yes"))),"Let's go for a picnic","Let's stay at home")		
12			
13			

3.12 SORTING

Very often there is a need to rearrange the rows or columns of your worksheet into a different order, numerical for data entries and alphabetical for text entries. Either of these can be displayed in ascending or descending alphabetical or numerical order. Most of the spreadsheets offer the facility of sorting rows or columns in several ways, as the examples in this section demonstrate.

Figure 3.31 shows a simple stock list. This can be sorted in a number of different ways but for our purposes it is first going to be sorted in ascending order of bin numbers, that is the entries in Column B. When sorting row by row on what is called a key column you must be sure that you do not include the column headings in the block of data to be sorted so you must specify, in this case, that you are sorting the contents of the block A3:D19 by the contents of column B. The result is shown in Figure 3.32. You will notice that this has the effect also of putting the contents of Column A in some sort of order as well, because similar types of things will go into the same bin. But if you look carefully you will see that the items are not in alphabetical order, which is not so much wrong as not exactly what we want. What in fact is needed is to sort mainly on the bin number but within each bin number the contents of column A could be put into alphabetical order. This is done by specifying that the secondary key column is column A, while the primary key column is column B. The result of sorting in this manner is shown in Figure 3.33.

Fig 3.31 *Stock list*

```
          A         B        C         D        E      F      G
1    Stock item    Bin      Cost    In stock
2    =========================================================
3    Bolts 1/4 in    3       0.12      200
4    Screws 1/2 in   5       0.05      124
5    Locks 2 lever   6       3.45       56
6    Bolts 1/2 in    6       0.05      231
7    Locks 4 lever   6      12.60       48
8    Nuts 1/2 in     3       0.04       12
9    Nuts 1/4 in     3       0.02      188
10   Screws 1/4 in   5       0.10      344
11   Nails 6 in      8       0.02      233
12   Screws 1/8 in   5       0.02      211
13   Spanners 14mm  10       1.20       90
14   Spanners 16mm  10       1.50       67
15   Nails 2 in      8       0.04      450
16   Spanners 12mm  10       1.10        4
17   Staples 5mm     2       0.01      500
18   Staples 3mm     2       0.01      456
19   Nails 5 in      8       0.09      244
20
A1: [W15] 'Stock item
25-Nov-88  12:45 AM                                          READY
```

Fig 3.32 *Sorted stock list by bin*

```
          A         B        C         D        E      F      G
1    Stock item    Bin      Cost    In stock
2    =========================================================
3    Staples 3mm     2       0.01      456
4    Staples 5mm     2       0.01      500
5    Nuts 1/2 in     3       0.04       12
6    Nuts 1/4 in     3       0.02      188
7    Bolts 1/4 in    3       0.12      200
8    Screws 1/8 in   5       0.02      211
9    Screws 1/2 in   5       0.05      124
10   Screws 1/4 in   5       0.10      344
11   Bolts 1/2 in    6       0.05      231
12   Locks 4 lever   6      12.60       48
13   Locks 2 lever   6       3.45       56
14   Nails 5 in      8       0.09      244
15   Nails 2 in      8       0.04      450
16   Nails 6 in      8       0.02      233
17   Spanners 14mm  10       1.20       90
18   Spanners 12mm  10       1.10        4
19   Spanners 16mm  10       1.50       67
20
A1: [W15] 'Stock item
25-Nov-88  12:50 AM                                          READY
```

Fig 3.33 *Sorted stock list by item name*

```
              A           B        C         D       E     F     G
 1    Stock item      Bin      Cost    In stock
 2    ==========================================
 3    Staples 3mm      2       0.01       456
 4    Staples 5mm      2       0.01       500
 5    Bolts 1/4 in     3       0.12       200
 6    Nuts 1/2 in      3       0.04        12
 7    Nuts 1/4 in      3       0.02       188
 8    Screws 1/2 in    5       0.05       124
 9    Screws 1/4 in    5       0.10       344
10    Screws 1/8 in    5       0.02       211
11    Bolts 1/2 in     6       0.05       231
12    Locks 2 lever    6       3.45        56
13    Locks 4 lever    6      12.60        48
14    Nails 2 in       8       0.04       450
15    Nails 5 in       8       0.09       244
16    Nails 6 in       8       0.02       233
17    Spanners 12mm   10       1.10         4
18    Spanners 14mm   10       1.20        90
19    Spanners 16mm   10       1.50        67
20
A1: [W15] 'Stock item
25-Nov-88  12:54 AM                                        READY
```

3.13 DATES

Very often there is a need not only to enter dates into a spreadsheet but to be able to manipulate these dates. For example it would be useful to be able to calculate the date 30 days after a particular date. If you merely wished to enter a date and then do nothing with it then it would be very simple to enter this as simple text. Be careful, however, to enter this date as text and prefix it with a quotation mark in most cases to avoid any confusion. Date functions tend to use a date serial number starting from a base date, often 1st January 1900, and calculate the date from the number of days from that date to the date in question. It is possible to extract from any date the day of the week, month of the year and year by using special functions. This also means that it is possible to find the number of days between two dates by subtracting one date from another. For example, Figure 3.34 shows the contents of a Lotus 1-2-3 spreadsheet with a number of date functions. The @NOW function gives a number that is the number of days from 1st January 1900 to today's date. The decimal part represents the time past midnight on the current day. By formatting the date in different ways the date can be presented in a variety of forms as shown in cells B1, C1 and D1. The @DATE function allows you to enter any date, the arguments being the year, month and day in that order. The date in cell A2 is displayed in the basic form and in a more readable format in cell B2. The difference between two dates is given in days in cell B3. By using the @INT function we can reduce this figure to the exact number of days. The functions @DAY, @MONTH and @YEAR will extract the day number, month number and year number from the dates. The actual display is shown in Figure 3.35. You should remember that if you use the @NOW, called TODAY by some spreadsheet programs, and save the sheet, its value will change from day to day as the current date changes.

Time functions can be dealt with in many spreadsheets using similar functions.

Fig 3.34 *Contents of spreadsheet showing date functions*

A5: @DAY(A2)

	A	B	C	D
1	@NOW	@NOW	@NOW	@NOW
2	@DATE(88,5,12)	@DATE(88,5,12)		
3	@MONTH(A2)	@INT(B2-B1)		
4	@YEAR(A2)			
5	@DAY(A2)			
6				
7				
8				
9				
10				
11				
12				
13				
14				
15				
16				
17				
18				
19				
20				

28-Apr-88   10:38 AM

72

Fig 3.35 *Spreadsheet display showing display from date functions*

A1: (G) @NOW

```
            A            B            C            D
1     32261.44338    28-Apr-88      28-Apr      04/28/88
2         32275      12-May-88
3             5           13
4            88
5            12
6
7
8
9
10
11
12
13
14
15
16
17
18
19
20
28-Apr-88   10:39 AM
```

3.14 MACRO FILES

There are often a large number of keystrokes involved when dealing with spreadsheets and very often these are repeated sets of operations. The keying-in of instructions is very prone to error and can often take a long time. It is very convenient to do the operation once only. Key it in, save the keystrokes in a special file and then whenever you want to "play back" the file all the operations will be carried out automatically. The file is known as a "macro" and the whole process is known as "executing a macro". Macros are normally entered as text, so that each command is not executed immediately. The whole command sequence stored in the macro is executed by a special macro command. The way that macros are entered and set into operation will differ from system to system. They all, however, work in the same manner.

The example shown next, written for the Lotus 1-2-3 spreadsheet, shows how every keystroke is recorded in a column as text in a Lotus worksheet. The sheet is saved and the range of the keystrokes is named as \a. This reminds the person using it that the way the macro is used is by pressing the **Alt** key and **a** simultaneously. All Lotus macros are set into motion by loading the sheet containing the macro into memory and then pressing the **Alt** key in conjunction with one other alphabetic key. Some spreadsheets call their macros "eXecute" files and have a special command to run them. However, they all work on the same premise that the keystrokes you would need to make are recorded and then played back when required. The Lotus macro is shown next:

```
\a        {goto}e1~
          Sales of PCs~
          {down}
          \-~
          {down}
          January~
          {down}
          February~
          {down}
          March~
          {down}
          April~
          {down}
          May~
          {down}
          June~
          {down}
          \=~
          {down}
          TOTAL:~
          {right}
          @sum(f3.f8)~
          {goto}f3~
          {?}
          {down}
          {?}
          {down}
          {?
          {down}
          {?}
          {down}
          {?}
```

74

{down}
{?}
{down}
\=~

The {down} command is the one that moves the cursor down one row, the ~ (tilde) sign is the equivalent of pressing the **Return** key and the {?} denotes the point where you have to enter data yourself. Everything else should be self explanatory. The final worksheet looks as shown in Figure 3.36. The numbers entered by you are those in the range F3:F8.

Fig 3.36 *Macro in a spreadsheet*

```
E9: \=                                                          READY

        A       B          C       D       E        F       G       H
1    \a      {goto}e1~                        Sales of PCs
2            Sales of PCs                      ----------
3            {down}                            January        45
4            \-~                               February       90
5            {down}                            March          43
6            January~                          April          56
7            {down}                            May            34
8            February~                         June           67
9            {down}                            ==================
10           March~                            TOTAL:        335
11           {down}
12           April~
13           {down}
14           May~
15           {down}
16           June~
17           {down}
18           \=~
19           {down}
20           TOTAL:~
25-Nov-88  01:09 AM
```

3.15 DATABASE APPLICATIONS

Many of the spreadsheet programs allow you to use a spreadsheet as a mini database. By this it is meant that you can enter sets of data row by row into your work-sheet and then select all those that have certain characteristics in common. For example if you have a list of all those people who have proficiency in certain word processors, their rate of pay and home base. Then it is possible to select all those that have the required features for a particular job. It should then be possible to extract the names of all those who are proficient in WordStar, charge under five pounds per hour and live in Watford.

When using a spreadsheet as a database the first thing to do is to create the data "file" as is shown in Figure 3.37. Each column must have a heading and you have to specify the extent of the whole table of entries. This is usually called the INPUT range. Away from the data you have to place the CRITERION range. This must contain some or all of the headings of the data table and beneath these are entered the tests to be applied. An example is shown in Figure 3.38 with the criterion range enclosed within the block of cells I1:N2. You should note that the contents of I2 contains a test of the rate which has to be less than 5 pounds and 50 pence and always uses the reference of the first cell below the heading (C2 in this case). Entries under the WordStar and WordCraft headings complete the set of criteria. What it does in fact is to produce a "sieve" through which the data on each line is "sifted". The successful entries in the data table are arranged to appear in the OUTPUT range which is the range starting with the row A13:H13. This is shown in Figure 3.39.

If you need to you can have more than one line of criteria and the second line provides an alternative "sieve" so that we are looking for either a person whose rate is less than 5.50 and is competent in both WordStar and WordCraft or a person whose base begins with the letter B and is competent in Word Perfect as shown in Figure 3.40. The results of this test are displayed on the screen shown in Figure 3.41. All the examples for this were produced using Lotus 1-2-3, but other spread-sheet programs use exactly the same type of structure.

Fig 3.37 *A data file*

A1: 'Reference   READY

	A	B	C	D	E	F	G	H
1	Reference	Name	'Rate	Base	W'Star	W'Perfect	W'Craft	M'Mate
2	AB456	Jones,K	5.85	Watford	Y	N	Y	N
3	DE342	Kenny,LK	4.50	Walton	Y	N	N	N
4	AS453	Morris,J	5.60	Harlow	Y	N	N	N
5	EE567	French,HG	4.95	Watford	Y	Y	N	Y
6	TR566	Lyons,W	5.25	Kilburn	Y	N	Y	Y
7	WS231	Craig,HJ	6.50	Bromley	Y	Y	Y	Y
8	BN675	Wilson,J	5.25	Bow	Y	Y	N	Y
9	BV783	Frost,D	4.35	Leyton	N	N	Y	N
10								
11								
12								
13								
14								
15								
16								
17								
18								
19								
20								

25-Nov-88   02:25 AM

Fig 3.38 *Criterion range*

I2: +C2<5.5   READY

	G	H	I	J	K	L	M	N
1	W'Craft	M'Mate	Rate	Base	W'Star	W'Perfect	W'Craft	M'Mate
2	Y	N		0	Y		Y	
3	N	N						
4	N	N						
5	N	Y						
6	Y	Y						
7	Y	Y						
8	N	Y						
9	Y	N						
10								
11								
12								
13								
14								
15								
16								
17								
18								
19								
20								

25-Nov-88   02:25 AM

Fig 3.39 *Selection made*

```
A1: 'Reference                                                    MENU
Input  Criterion  Output  Find  Extract  Unique  Delete  Reset  Quit
Copy all records that match criteria to Output range
         A         B       C       D        E        F         G       H
1   Reference   Name    Rate     Base  ·  W'Star   W'PerfectW'Craft  M'Mate
2   AB456      Jones,K   5.85  Watford   Y        N         Y       N
3   DE342      Kenny,LK  4.50  Walton    Y        N         N       N
4   AS453      Morris,J  5.60  Harlow    Y        Y         N       N
5   EE567      French,HG 4.95  Watford   Y        N         N       Y
6   TR566      Lyons,W   5.25  Kilburn   Y        N         Y       Y
7   WS231      Craig,HJ  6.50  Bromley   Y        Y         Y       Y
8   BN675      Wilson,J  5.25  Bow       Y        Y         N       Y
9   BV783      Frost,D   4.35  Leyton    N        N         Y       N
10
11
12
13  Reference   Name    Rate     Base     W'Star   W'PerfectW'Craft  M'Mate
14  TR566      Lyons,W   5.25  Kilburn    Y        N         Y       Y
15
16
17
18
19
20
25-Nov-88  02:26 AM
```

Fig 3.40 *Alternative criterion*

```
N1: 'M'Mate                                                       READY

         G         H       I        J        K        L        M       N
1   W'Craft   M'Mate    Rate     Base     W'Star   W'PerfectW'Craft  M'Mate
2   Y        N                O  Y                          Y
3   N        N                   B*           Y
4   N        N
5   N        Y
6   Y        Y
7   Y        Y
8   N        Y
9   Y        N
10
11
12
13  W'Craft   M'Mate
14  Y        Y
15  Y        Y
16  N        Y
17
18
19
20
25-Nov-88  02:29 AM
```

78

Fig 3.41 *New selection made*

SUMMARY

1. A spreadsheet formula relates the contents of cells in the sheet by some mathematical expression and displays the answer to the calculation in the cell containing the formula.

2. A cell or group of cells can be formatted to display their contents in a number of ways to suit you. This does not affect the contents of the cells in any way.

3. One or more row or column can be inserted into your worksheet anywhere in it. Any cells that are moved as a result of this are automatically adjusted.

4. A cell entry, particularly a formula, can be protected from accidental erasure or overwriting. The contents of cells can be hidden from view either by giving a command not to display their contents or by shrinking the width of a column to zero. This again does not affect the contents of the cells.

5. A cell or block of cells can be copied to another part of the sheet and if necessary the formulas

contained in the cells are adjusted accordingly. Blocks of cells can also be moved from one part of the sheet to another.

6. A spreadsheet look-up function can be used to look up numbers in a table for such things as rates of discount, rates of commission or rates of tax associated with certain ranges - or bands - of numbers.

7. For very large sheets horizontal or vertical titles can be "frozen" so that they remain in place while the rest of the sheet scrolls.

8. A worksheet can be divided into two windows so that you can examine two parts of the sheet at the same time.

9. Recalculation usually takes place in natural order, column by column or row by row.

10. Be careful of circular references where either directly or indirectly a cell refers to itself. It might be by design, but usually it is by accident.

11. Spreadsheets can be used as small databases from which information can be extracted.

12. Logical decisions can be made using IF together with AND, OR and NOT.

13. Macro files can be created so that a large number of keystrokes can be performed automatically and correctly by a simple instruction.

14. The contents of a worksheet can be sorted by row or by column, alphabetically or numerically in ascending or descending order.

15. Functions exist that can manipulate both dates and times.

GRAPHS AND CHARTS

Most of the spreadsheet programs now available allow you to display data held on your worksheet in a number of graphical forms both on the screen or in "hard copy" produced by a printer or a plotter. Not every computer has the facility to display graphs on the screen and graphs cannot be plotted with a daisywheel printer; you need either a dot matrix printer or a laser printer in order to do this. These are points you should check with your supplier before purchasing a spreadsheet program. Ask to see it demonstrated doing the things you require before you finally take the plunge!

The types of graphs plotted by the programs can be of the following types:

1. Bar charts
2. Stacked bar charts
3. Line graphs
4. Pie charts
5. X-Y graphs
6. Hi-Lo charts

The graphs can be annotated with titles, both general and for each axis, and legends, usually with a variety of fonts to choose from. Usually one graph is printed at a time but there are a few programs that allow you not only to display more than one graph on the screen at one time but also to print them on the same sheet of paper.

When you have the spreadsheet data you require to display you have to define a number of things. The first of these is the range of data to be plotted. This may be a simple list of numbers or, if you want to display several sets of numbers for comparison on the same graph, then each range is entered as a separate "variable".

Having defined the range(s) of variables you need to specify the information to go on your graph apart from purely numerical information. This involves selecting titles for the graph itself and titles for the axes. The horizontal axis is known as the "X" or "Time" axis while the vertical axis is known as the "Y" axis. When you have several variables plotted on the same graph you will need to be able to distinguish between them. This is done usually by defining the "legend" which is the key to the type of shading done on bar charts and pie charts or the symbol that is used to identify the points on a line graph. If you draw a pie chart then it is possible to "explode" (or pull out) one or more segments of the pie in order to add emphasis.

The spreadsheet programs will usually scale the graph automatically for you so that it fits easily into the available space. If you wish, however, you can decide on your own scaling for the axes.

A set of typefaces, or fonts, are available for the display of the titles so that you can choose which typeface is best suited to your style. You can also choose the density of the printing; the greater the print density the blacker the output but it will take longer to print on a dot matrix printer.

The examples that follow will illustrate the types of graph and typefaces available. First of all Figure 4.1 shows the spreadsheet from which the first few examples are taken. Figure 4.2 shows the information taken from the spreadsheet and displayed by means of a line graph; note the legend at the top right-hand corner of the graph. Figure 4.3 shows the same information displayed on a bar chart. The switch from one type of graph to another is very quick and easy. All that has to be done is to return to the graph menu and change the graph type. All the information regarding where the data is to be found on the worksheet remains.

Fig 4.1 *Spreadsheet data for graphing*

	A || B || C || D || E || F
1	QX Computers Ltd					
2						
3	Sales in 1987 - (000s)					
4						
5		PCs		Software	Other	Services
6	1st Quarter	13.5		3.3		1.56
7	2nd Quarter	15.5		2.7		3.99
8	3rd Quarter	12.4		1.8		1.2
9	4th Quarter	21.9		1.7		1.5

Fig 4.2 *Line graph from data*

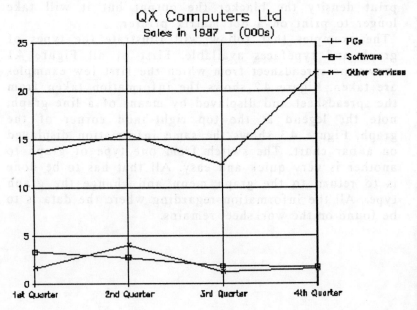

QX Computers Ltd
Sales in 1987 - (000s)

Fig 4.3 *Bar chart from data*

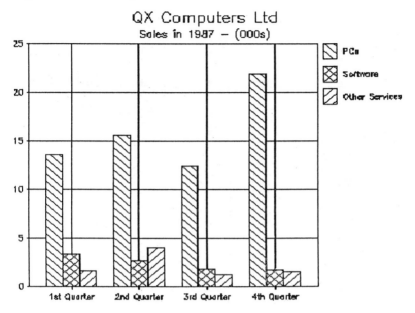

QX Computers Ltd
Sales in 1987 — (000s)

When you save a worksheet containing graph information all this is stored away as well so that when you recall the sheet into memory you can update the information it contains and plot the graph at once. Figure 4.4 shows the same information again, but displayed on a stacked bar chart. Figure 4.5 shows the information provided by SuperCalc3 regarding the parameters being used to plot the graph shown in Figure 4.2.

One column of data only, of course, can be used in the plotting of a pie chart and the first column of data in our example worksheet has been used to provide the pie chart shown in Figure 4.6. Any or all of the "slices" of a pie chart can be "exploded" out for greater emphasis and Figure 4.7 shows the effect of exploding one of the segments. The percentages displayed beside each segment of the chart are automatically calculated and displayed without any prompting by you.

Fig 4.4 *Stacked bar chart from data*

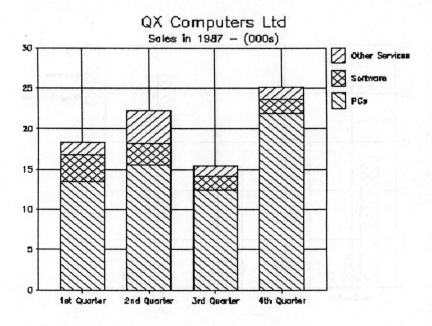

Fig 4.5 *SuperCalc graph specification*

```
Current Graph (#1) -> Bar   Current Device -> EPSON LX80, FX85 Printer

HEADINGS:                        SCALING:
Main:   (B1)                     Y-Axis: Auto
Sub:    (B3)                     X-Axis: Auto
X-Axis: (empty)
Y-Axis: (empty)

TIME LABELS: (A6:A9)

    Data        Pt-Labels      Var-Labels       FORMATS:
A:  (C6:C9)     (empty)        (C5)             Axis:
B:  (D6:D9)     (empty)        (D5)             Time:
C:  (E6:E9)     (empty)        (E5)             Var:
D:  (empty)     (empty)        (E9)             Point:
E:  (empty)     (empty)        (empty)          % :
F:  (empty)     (empty)        (empty)
G:  (empty)     (empty)        (empty)
H:  (empty)     (empty)        (empty)
I:  (empty)     (empty)        (empty)
J:  (empty)     (empty)        (empty)

PIE EXPLOSION: None                    MODE: One Variable (A)
F1 or <?> for AnswerScreen.
MENU  View the current graph    F3:Graphs List
```

Fig 4.6 *Pie chart from data*

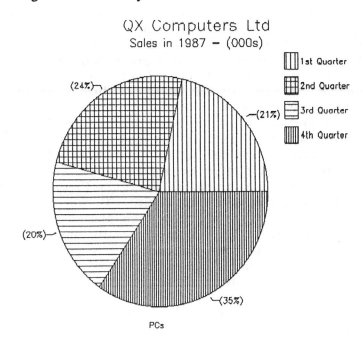

Fig 4.7 *Pie chart - one segment exploded*

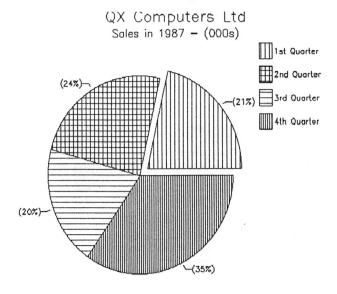

Not all spreadsheet programs are capable of displaying more than one graph on the same screen or sheet of paper. Logistix, however, is one that does and Figure 4.8 shows the information taken from our worksheet by this program and displayed as three graphs side by side producing a very easy way of comparing the information. This program, as you will see later, can display up to four graphs at one time.

X-Y graphs are graphs of the type where one set of numbers, called the "dependent" set and plotted vertically, are related to another set of numbers called the "independent" set and plotted horizontally. The information leading to an X-Y graph, as shown in Figure 4.9, can lead to the graph shown in Figure 4.10 where you will notice that the X points have been plotted not at regular intervals but as they occur naturally along the scale. If the graph had been plotted as a line graph the result would have been as shown in Figure 4.11. X-Y graphs are used when plotting mathematical graphs.

Fig 4.8 *Logistix pie charts*

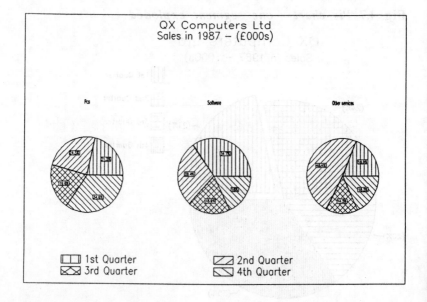

Fig 4.9 *Data for X-Y graph*

```
            A           B          C         D         E         F         G         H
1    X                Y
2            1                3
3            2.3              7
4            4                14
5            4.5              16
6            6.7              19
7            7                20
8            9.1              28
9            11.5             35
10           12               40
11           15.6             50
12
13
14
15
16
17
18
19
20
B1:  'Y
25-Nov-88   03:22 AM                                                    READY
```

Fig 4.10 *Correct X-Y graph from data*

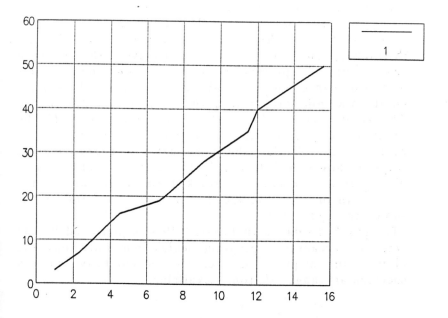

Fig 4.11 *Line graph from data*

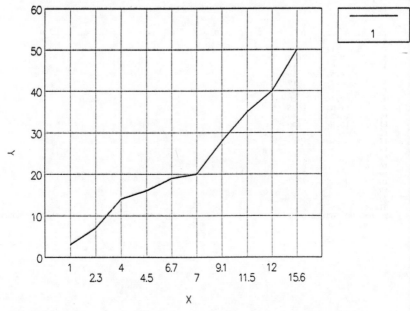

Hi-Lo graphs are used for plotting such information as stock market fluctuations. The worksheet shown in Figure 4.12 shows details of the share movements for several companies. Figure 4.13 lists the variables used to produce the display shown in Figure 4.14.

The Logistix worksheet illustrated in Figure 4.15 contains not only the data to be displayed but also the instructions on how it is to be displayed, this being a feature of this particular program. From the Logistix menu you can choose the position on the page of each pie chart (**pia**, **pib**, etc. define the position on the page). The final result looks as shown in Figure 4.16. If the graph plotting instructions are modified on the worksheet you can display the same data in four different ways as shown in Figure 4.17. The data is displayed as a pie chart, a bar chart, a stacked bar chart and a pie chart with one slice exploded. The modified worksheet is shown in Figure 4.18.

The graph displayed in Figure 4.19 was produced by the Quattro spreadsheet program which not only has the ability to display bar charts horizontally has a spectacular range of fonts available.

Fig 4.12 *Data for Hi-Lo graph*

!	A	!!	B	!!	C	!!	D	!!	E	!!	F	!!	G	!
1	Share movement 1988		High		Low		March		June		Sept		Dec	
2														
3	Jones Industries Ord 50p		450		123		434		444		423		125	
4	QX Computers 5% Pref		112		79		110		95		87		81	
5	Shark Loan Co		450		90		390		300		250		100	
6	Dough Bakeries Ltd		56		25		54		45		33		26	
7	Frogspawn Plc		98		16		97		80		60		19	

Fig 4.13 *Graph specification for Hi-Lo graph*

Current Graph (£1) -> Hi-Lo   Current Device -> IBM Graphics Printer

```
HEADINGS:                    SCALING:
Main:    (A1)                Y-Axis: Auto
Sub:     (empty)            X-Axis: Auto
X-Axis:  (empty)
Y-Axis:  (empty)

TIME LABELS: (empty)

       Data         Pt-Labels       Var-Labels       FORMATS:
A:  (B3:B7)         (empty)         (G1)             Axis:
B:  (C3:C7)         (empty)         (C1)             Time:
C:  (D3:D7)         (empty)         (D1)             Var:
D:  (E3:E7)         (empty)         (E1)             Point:
E:  (F3:F7)         (empty)         (F1)             % :
F:  (G3:G7)         (empty)         (empty)
G:  (empty)         (empty)         (empty)
H:  (empty)         (empty)         (empty)
I:  (empty)         (empty)         (empty)
J:  (empty)         (empty)         (empty)

PIE EXPLOSION: None              MODE: One Variable (A)
F1 or <?> for AnswerScreen.
MENU  View the current graph  F3:Graphs List
```

Fig 4.14 *Hi-Lo graph*

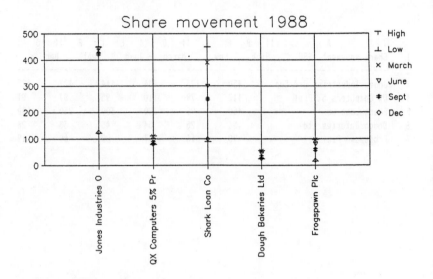

Fig 4.15 *Data for a set of pie charts*

```
       |   A    |        B          |   C
 1   tia f7   QX Computers Ltd
 2   tib f7   Sales in 1987 (#000s)
 3   tic f7   1st Quarter
 4   pia
 5   pie      Pcs                    13.5
 6   pie      Software                3.3
 7   pie      Other services         1.56
 8
 9   tia f7   QX Computers Ltd
10   tib f7   Sales in 1987 (#000s)
11   tic f7   2nd Quarter
12   pib
13   pie      Pcs                    15.5
14   pie      Software                2.7
15   pie      Other services         3.99
16
17   tia f7   QX Computers Ltd
18   tib f7   Sales in 1987 (#000s)
19   tic f7   3rd Quarter
20   pic
21   pie      Pcs                    12.4
22   pie      Software                1.8
23   pie      Other services         1.2
24
25   tia f7   QX Computers Ltd
26   tib f7   Sales in 1987 (#000s)
27   tic f7   4th Quarter
28   pic
29   pie      Pcs                    21.9
30   pie      Software                1.7
31   pie      Other services         1.5
```

Fig 4.16 *Set of pie charts*

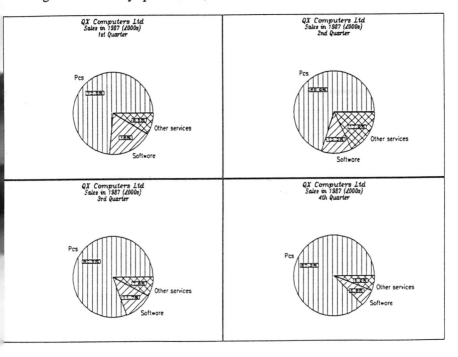

Fig 4.17 *Different graphs plotted together*

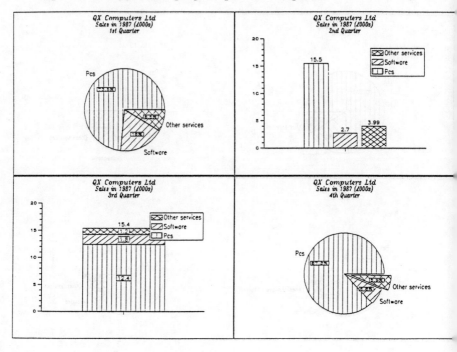

Fig 4.18 *Data for set of different graphs*

```
   |  A   |     B        |  C

 1  tia f7    QX Computers Ltd
 2  tib f7    Sales in 1987 (#000s)
 3  tic f7    1st Quarter
 4  pia
 5  pie       Pcs                 13.5
 6  pie       Software             3.3
 7  pie       Other services       1.56
 8
 9  tia f7    QX Computers Ltd
10  tib f7    Sales in 1987 (#000s)
11  tic f7    2nd Quarter
12  bvc an
13  bar       Pcs                 15.5
14  bar       Software             2.7
15  bar       Other services       3.99
16  lgd p3 bx
17
18  tia f7    QX Computers Ltd
19  tib f7    Sales in 1987 (#000s)
20  tic f7    3rd Quarter
21  bvs an
22  bar       Pcs                 12.4
23  bar       Software             1.8
24  bar       Other services       1.2
25  lgd p3 bx
26
27
28  tia f7    QX Computers Ltd
29  tib f7    Sales in 1987 (#000s)
30  tic f7    4th Quarter
31  pic
32  pie       Pcs                 21.9
33  pie       Software             1.7
34  pie ex    Other services       1.5
```

Fig 4.19 *Graph plotted by Quattro*

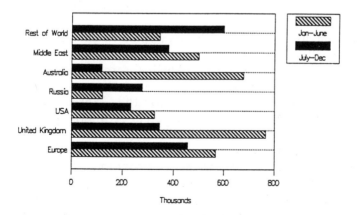

𝕴nternational 𝕮at—flaps 𝕴nr

𝔖ales

INTEGRATED PACKAGES

5.1 WORD PROCESSORS, DATABASES AND SPREADSHEETS

There are now a number of programs available that combine all the features of several different programs. They allow a user to incorporate data from a spreadsheet very simply into a report generated by a word processor without a lot of changing of programs. Popular programs of this type are Symphony, Framework and Ability Plus.

Programs of this type often tend to adopt the "desktop" approach to computing. This turns your screen into a make-believe desk with filing cabinets, wastepaper baskets and scribbling pads. Documents are filed away in, and retrieved from, a "drawer" in the "filing cabinet" and consigned to the "waste bin" when discarded. By a simple sequence of keystrokes you can create a spreadsheet, integrate it with other documents, create graphs and manipulate the data it contains in all manner of ways.

The program used to create the examples in this chapter was Ability Plus.

Figure 5.1 shows the opening Ability screen. You can see how choices can be made for the operation you wish to carry out. Move the cursor to the "Spreadsheet" column and the <<New>> option selected. A blank spreadsheet is then displayed as shown in Figure 5.2. All the commands and functions available are very similar to those used in other spreadsheet programs and the worksheet shown in Figure 5.3 was very quickly created.

One of the great features of such a program is that having created a spreadsheet not only can you draw graphs from it very easily but you can also include the worksheet and the graphs into a single document produced by the word processing part of the program. In addition, the spreadsheet and the graph can be kept active while they are in the document. This means that if you wish to change any data in the sheet it will recalculate and because you can link a worksheet with a graph any changes made in the sheet data will cause the graph to be redrawn as well. Another useful feature of these programs is that similar commands are used in all parts of the program, so that the commands used in the manipulation of a spreadsheet are similar to those in the database and the word processor.

A graph drawn from the spreadsheet data is shown in Figure 5.4 and all three combined in a single document are shown in Figure 5.5. If you have a plotter you can arrange for graphs to be drawn in any one of four quadrants of the paper. The latest version of SuperCalc, SuperCalc4, allows you to choose where on the page your graph is to be plotted.

Fig 5.1 *Ability opening screen*

```
                        <<<<     Ability Plus v1.0     >>>>

DATABASE   SPREADSHEET   GRAPH      WRITE    COMMUNICATE   PROGRAMS      FILES

<<New>>    <<New>>     <<New>>    <<New>>    <<New>>                    [A:]
ADDRESS      ADDR      GRAPH1     READ_ME                              [B:]
           CASHFLOW     GRAPH2     REPORT                              [C:]
            SALES                                                      <..>
                                                                   CONFIG.SYS






                                                      28% Free
C:\ABILITY
Please point at a file with arrow keys and press RETURN
F1 - Help        F3 - Goto        F5 - Pickup           F9 - Flip
F2 - Commands                                           F10 - Done
```

Fig 5.2 *Blank Ability spreadsheet*

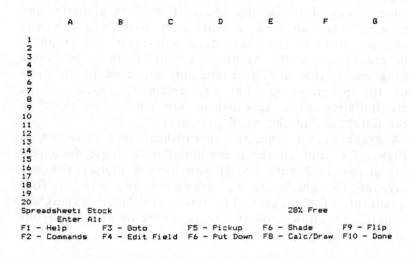

```
          A       B       C       D       E       F       G
 1
 2
 3
 4
 5
 6
 7
 8
 9
10
11
12
13
14
15
16
17
18
19
20
Spreadsheet: Stock                           28% Free
     Enter A1:
F1 - Help      F3 - Goto       F5 - Pickup     F6 - Shade      F9 - Flip
F2 - Commands  F4 - Edit Field F6 - Put Down   F8 - Calc/Draw  F10 - Done
```

Fig 5.3 *Ability spreadsheet*

Sales in 1988 - (Pounds - '000s)

	Pcs	Software	Other Services
1st Quarter	13.5	3.3	1.56
2nd Quarter	15.5	2.7	3.99
3rd Quarter	12.4	1.8	1.2
4th Quarter	21.9	1.7	1.5

Fig 5.4 *Graph from Ability spreadsheet*

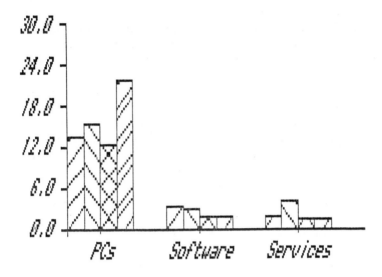

Sales in £000s

Fig 5.5 *Complete document produced by Ability*

QX Computers Ltd.

From the table below you can see that the general trend of
business has been good. PC sales have increased but the sales of
software have remained constant. Other services such as training
and sales of computer supplies have been too variable every
effort must be made to increase these in the coming year.

Sales in 1988 - (Pounds - '000s)

	Pcs	Software	Other Services
1st Quarter	13.5	3.3	1.56
2nd Quarter	15.5	2.7	3.99
3rd Quarter	12.4	1.8	1.2
4th Quarter	21.9	1.7	1.5

This is clearly shown in the following graph.

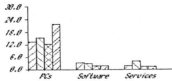

Sales in £000s

5.2 IMPORTING AND EXPORTING SPREADSHEETS

The ease with which spreadsheets can be moved about between different programs varies from program to program. For example Lotus 1-2-3 has a feature called **Translate** which enables worksheets prepared in alien formats to be converted into Lotus sheets and Lotus sheets to be converted into other formats. It also applies the translation process to and from database files for dBASE II and dBASE III. Early versions of SuperCalc use a program called **SDI** (**Super Data Interchange**) that will perform a similar function. Logistix on the other hand will quite simply read a Lotus, SuperCalc or dBASE file without having to call upon a separate translation program. Some examples of these and other import/export operations follow.

Our starting point is a database file that was created using the dBASE III program. It was called ADDRESS.DBF. First of all it was converted into what is called a "comma separated variable" file. This means that each field of the records in the file was copied into a text file called ADDRESS.TXT and was separated from its neighbour by a comma. This was done by the dBASE III program by the commands

use address

copy to address delimited

The resulting file looks as shown in Figure 5.6. Then the dBASE program was closed down and the SDI program used. This arranges for a file in the comma separated format to be converted into SuperCalc format. The resulting file is called ADDRESS.CAL and on the Super-Calc spreadsheet it looks as shown in Figure 5.7. That was how SuperCalc could deal with it.

To convert the same database file into Lotus 1-2-3 format you must use the Lotus Translate program. This is selected from the main Lotus menu and you are asked for the format of the file to be imported, dBASE III in this case, and its name. Then you have to specify the Lotus format, depending on the version of the program you have and you then leave the program to do the rest. The resulting screen when Lotus 1-2-3 finally gets hold of the file is as shown in Figure 5.8. You should notice

Fig 5.6 *Text file from dBASE*

```
"F0000001","Fellowes","K.M.","Miss","The Haven","Cross St.","Haverham","YT6 7TY"
"T0000001","Thomas","O.P.","Ms","21 Fleet Rd","Weyborn","Norfolk","NR5 6TY"
"M0000001","Masters","K.H.","Mr","Flat 3","32 Cross Rd","Empingham","EM7 9OP"
"K0000001","Kenwood","A.G.","Mr","21a Field Rd","Kenton","Middx","ME5 2WS"
"A0000001","Allows","M.N.","Miss","78 Tide St","Hapton","Gloucs","GL4 3ED"
"K0000002","Katworthy","K.","Mr","29 Church Rd","Hallon","Cambs","CB4 5RT"
"J0000001","Johnson","M.","Ms","77a The Parade","Witham","Worcs","WA4 5QS"
"B0000001","Barlow","C.","Ch.Ins","6 The Pool","Northwich","Cheshire","L89 5TY"
"D0000001","Donaldson","I.V.","Miss","1 High St","Wallam","Salop","WA2 9PK"
"F0000002","Francis","H.L.","Mr","65 Grove Street","Edgington","Notts","NG2 4RT"
"D0000005","Davis","T.H.","Mrs","23 East Street","Stamford","Lincs","PE9 5TR"
"H0000001","Harris","G.L.J.","Mr","Barns","East on the Hil","Stamford","Pe8 7YT"
```

Fig 5.7 *File after translation into SuperCalc*

	A	B	C	D	E	F	G	H
1	F0000001	Fellowes	K.M.	Miss	The Haven	Cross St.	Haverham	YT6 7TY
2	T0000001	Thomas	O.P.	Ms	21 Fleet	Weyborn	Norfolk	NR5 6TY
3	M0000001	Masters	K.H.	Mr	Flat 3	32 Cross	Empingham	EM7 9OP
4	K0000001	Kenwood	A.G.	Mr	21a Field	Kenton	Middx	ME5 2WS
5	A0000001	Allows	M.N.	Miss	78 Tide S	Hapton	Gloucs	GL4 3ED
6	K0000002	Katworthy	K.	Mr	29 Church	Hallon	Cambs	CB4 5RT
7	J0000001	Johnson	M.	Ms	77a The P	Witham	Worcs	WA4 5QS
8	B0000001	Barlow	C.	Ch.Ins	6 The Poo	Northwich	Cheshire	L89 5TY
9	D0000001	Donaldson	I.V.	Miss	1 High St	Wallam	Salop	WA2 9PK
10	F0000002	Francis	H.L.	Mr	65 Grove	Edgington	Notts	NG2 4RT
11	D0000005	Davis	T.H.	Mrs	23 East S	Stamford	Lincs	PE9 5TR
12	H0000001	Harris	G.L.J.	Mr	Barns	East on t	Stamford	Pe8 7YT

that in this case Lotus has preserved the column headings, which were the field names in the original file, and displayed them at the head of each column. As well as this the width of each field has been set to the width of the original field. Lotus also has a file import option directly from the worksheet but it will only import text, one line per cell, or numbers. This could cause problems. The safest way to import external data files is through the Translate option.

The Logistix program works in an even more direct manner since when you come to load a file you are able to specify the source format of the file. The most common choices being AT dBase (Ashton-Tate dBase), 1-2-3 (Lotus 1-2-3 version 1 only) and SC (SuperCalc). The file is then read in and displayed as shown in Figure 5.9. Again the column headings are taken from the original field names and the widths of the columns are set to the original field widths.

Ability being an integrated program allows transfer between its own database and spreadsheet sections. With this program the imported file is read into an Ability database file, one record of which is shown in Figure 5.10. The appearance of the record is exactly the same as when you display it in its original form. Then the file is "picked up" and then "put down" into a spreadsheet with the final result as shown in Figure 5.11. Ability does not have to be told the format of the original file to be imported, it will sense that from the file format.

Although Boeing Calc looks very similar to Lotus 1-2-3 its file importation is very direct and will read a sheet in Lotus format without a special conversion program being invoked.

Fig 5.8 *File after importation into Lotus 1-2-3*

CUSTREF SURNAME	INITIA	TITLE	ADDRESS1	ADDRESS2
F0000001Fellowes	K.M.	Miss	The Haven	Cross St.
T0000001Thomas	O.P.	Ms	21 Fleet Rd	Weyborn
M0000001Masters	K.H.	Mr	Flat 3	32 Cross Rd
K0000001Kenwood	A.G.	Mr	21a Field Rd	Kenton
A0000001Allows	M.N.	Miss	78 Tide St	Hapton
K0000002Katworthy	K.	Mr	29 Church Rd	Hallon
J0000001Johnson	M.	Ms	77a The Parade	Witham
B0000001Barlow	C.	Ch.Inso	The Pool	Northwich
D0000001Donaldson	I.V.	Miss	1 High St	Wallam
F0000002Francis	H.L.	Mr	65 Grove Street	Edgington
D0000005Davis	T.H.	Mrs	23 East Street	Stamford
H0000001Harris	G.L.J.	Mr	Barns	East on the Hil

Fig 5.9 *File after importation into Logistix*

	A	B	C	D	E	F	G	H
1	CUSTREF	SURNAME	INITIALS	TITLE	ADDRESS1	ADDRESS2	ADDRESS3	POSTCODE
2	F0000001	Fellowes	K.M.	Miss	The Have	Cross St	Haverham	YT6 7TY
3	T0000001	Thomas	O.P.	Ms	21 Fleet	Weyborn	Norfolk	NR5 6TY
4	M0000001	Masters	K.H.	Mr	Flat 3	32 Cross	Empingha	EM7 9OP
5	K0000001	Kenwood	A.G.	Mr	21a Fiel	Kenton	Middx	ME5 2WS
6	A0000001	Allows	M.N.	Miss	78 Tide	Hapton	Gloucs	GL4 3ED
7	K0000002	Katworth	K.	Mr	29 Churc	Hallon	Cambs	CB4 5RT
8	J0000001	Johnson	M.	Ms	77a The	Witham	Worcs	WA4 5QS
9	B0000001	Barlow	C.	Ch.Ins	6 The Po	Northwic	Cheshire	L89 5TY
10	D0000001	Donaldso	I.V.	Miss	1 High S	Wallam	Salop	WA2 9PK
11	F0000002	Francis	H.L.	Mr	65 Grove	Edgingto	Notts	NG2 4RT
12	D0000005	Davis	T.H.	Mrs	23 East	Stamford	Lincs	PE9 5TR
13	H0000001	Harris	G.L.J.	Mr	Barns	East on	Stamford	FeB 7YT

Fig 5.10 *One record of file imported into Ability*

```
CUSTREF      F0000001
SURNAME      Fellowes
INITIALS     K.M.
TITLE        Miss
ADDRESS1     The Haven
ADDRESS2     Cross St.
ADDRESS3     Haverham
POSTCODE     YT6 7TY
```

```
DB ADDRESS; Browse          Form1                 28% Free
Enter ADDRESS3: Haverham
F1 - Help        F3 - Goto        F5 - Pickup                   F9 - Flip
F2 - Commands    F4 - Edit Field  F6 - Put Down  FS - Calc/Draw  F10 - Done
```

Fig 5.11 *File read into Ability spreadsheet*

```
F0000001 Fellowes    K.M.   Miss     The Haven        Cross St.        Have
T0000001 Thomas      O.P.   Ms       21 Fleet Rd      Weyborn          Norf
M0000001 Masters     K.H.   Mr       Flat 3           32 Cross Rd      Empi
K0000001 Kenwood     A.G.   Mr       21a Field Rd     Kenton           Midd
A0000001 Allows      M.N.   Miss     78 Tide St       Hapton           Glou
K0000002 Katworthy   K.     Mr       29 Church Rd     Hallon           Camb
J0000001 Johnson     M.     Ms       77a The Parade   Witham           Worc
B0000001 Barlow      C.     Ch.Ins   6 The Pool       Northwich        Ches
D0000001 Donaldson   I.V.   Miss     1 High St        Wallam           Salo
F0000002 Francis     H.L.   Mr       65 Grove Street  Edgington        Nott
D0000005 Davis       T.H.   Mrs      23 East Street   Stamford         Linc
H0000001 Harris      G.L.J. Mr       Barns            East on the Hil  Stam
```

```
       Enter A13:
F1 - Help        F3 - Goto        F5 - Pick Up     F7 - Shade     F9 - Flip
F2 - Commands    F4 - Edit Field  F6 - Put Down    F8 - Calc/Draw  F10 - Done
```

Exporting a file usually follows similar lines to the importing of a file. Sometimes, however, you may be using a program that does not list the target program among the formats available. Very often the day can be saved by using DIF (Date Interchange Format) files. These files are in a universally accepted format and enable, for example, a file stored in Logistix format to be read into a Boeing Calc file. This was done with our example file with the beginning of the DIF file created by Logistix shown in Figure 5.12. Boeing Calc can then read the DIF file and display it. You should notice that the file contains header information about the structure of the file followed by the contents of the file itself row by row.

Fig 5.12 *DIF file contents*

TABLE	**−1,0**	**1,0**
0,1	**BOT**	**"ADDRESS2"**
■■	**1,0**	**1,0**
VECTORS	**"CUSTREF"**	**"ADDRESS3"**
0,8	**1,0**	**1,0**
■■	**"SURNAME"**	**"POSTCODE"**
TUPLES	**1,0**	**−1,0**
0,16	**"INITIALS"**	**BOT**
■■	**1,0**	**1,0**
DATA	**"TITLE"**	**"F0000001"**
0,0	**1,0**	**1,0**
■■	**"ADDRESS1"**	**"Fellowes"**

1,0	**1,0**	**1,0**
■■	■■	■■
1,0	**1,0**	**1,0**
■■	■■	■■
1,0	**−1,0**	**1,0**
■■	**BOT**	■■
1,0	**1,0**	**1,0**
■■	■■	■■
1,0	**1,0**	**1,0**
■■	■■	■■
1,0	**1,0**	**−1,0**
■■	■■	**EOD**

HOW TO DO ...

This chapter goes into detail to describe how certain important operations are performed using a spreadsheet program. As you will see, each example contains a list of the spreadsheet features used to produce each of the examples. The actual spreadsheet is shown together with the final result that is output on your printer or screen.

6.1 A CASHFLOW

In order to produce a cashflow worksheet you must be able to:

1. Sum sets of figures
2. Replicate formulas
3. Change the width of columns
4. Format blocks of entries so that they are displayed in money format - i.e. xxx,xxx.xx preferably with a currency symbol preceding the amount and with negative amounts enclosed in brackets
5. Draw continuous lines across the screen

If you wish to display the information graphically you must also be able to:

6. Define a graph type
7. Define the data ranges
8. Define headings
9. Define the text to be written at the foot of the graph
10. Define the content of the legend

The display for a cashflow is shown in Figure 6.1.1. The contents of the worksheet are shown in Figure 6.1.2 and a graph drawn from the data is shown in Figure 6.1.3.

This worksheet and graph were produced using SuperCalc.

Fig 6.1.1 *Cashflow spreadsheet*

Software Trainers Cashflow Forecast

Month:	Dec '87 Forecast	Jan '88 Forecast	Feb '88 Forecast	Mar '88 Forecast	Apr '88 Forecast	May '88 Forecast	Dec '87 Actual	Jan '88 Actual	Feb '88 Actual	Mar '88 Actual	Apr '88 Actual	May '88 Actual
RECEIPTS - General	3240.00	2000.00	2000.00	2000.00	2000.00	2000.00	3361.11	2015.42	1885.49	3674.30	2000.00	2000.00
RECEIPTS Deposit A/C				360.00	360.00	360.00			1000.00	2000.00	360.00	360.00
RECEIPTS - Courses				1440.00	1440.00	1440.00			332.75	1444.31	1440.00	1440.00
TOTAL RECEIPTS	3240.00	2000.00	2000.00	3800.00	3800.00	3800.00	3361.11	2015.42	3218.24	7118.61	3800.00	3800.00
PAYMENTS												
Advertising	200.00	200.00	150.00	150.00	150.00	150.00	162.86	423.65	150.00	150.00	150.00	150.00
Stationery			50.00	50.00	50.00	50.00			50.00	50.00	50.00	50.00
To creditors	65.00	65.00	65.00	65.00	65.00	65.00	65.00	65.00	65.00	65.00	65.00	65.00
Wages & Salaries	200.00	200.00	200.00	200.00	200.00	200.00	202.00	200.00	200.00	200.00	200.00	200.00
Rent/Rates		160.00			400.00			257.94			400.00	
Electricity	25.00	25.00	25.00	25.00	25.00	25.00	.00	10.24	25.00	25.00	25.00	25.00
Transport - Car	96.00	96.00	96.00	96.00	96.00	96.00	96.00	96.00	96.00	96.00	96.00	96.00
Transport - Petrol	80.00	80.00	80.00	80.00	80.00	80.00	119.66	95.36	80.00	80.00	80.00	80.00
Equipment Leasing	100.00	100.00	100.00	460.00	460.00	460.00	100.00	100.00	100.00	556.00	460.00	460.00
Telephone	40.00	40.00	40.00	40.00	40.00	40.00	193.59	52.33	40.00	311.00	40.00	40.00
Postage	20.00	20.00	20.00	20.00	20.00	20.00	18.07	9.72	20.00	20.00	20.00	20.00
VAT		400.00			600.00			578.03			600.00	
Drawings	1400.00	1400.00	1400.00	1400.00	2100.00	2100.00	2800.00		1400.00	1900.00	2100.00	2100.00
Petty Cash	50.00	50.00	50.00	50.00	50.00	50.00	51.73	12.70	50.00	50.00	50.00	50.00
TOTAL EXPENSES	2276.00	2836.00	2276.00	2636.00	4336.00	3336.00	3808.91	1900.97	2276.00	3503.00	4336.00	3336.00
NET	964.00	(836.00)	(276.00)	1,164.00	(536.00)	464.00	(447.80)	114.45	942.24	3,615.61	(536.00)	464.00
Balance from previous month	(1,800.00)	(836.00)	(1,672.00)	(1,948.00)	(784.00)	(1,320.00)	(1,800.00)	(2,247.80)	(2,133.35)	(1,191.11)	2,424.50	1,888.50
Net balance	(836.00)	(1,672.00)	(1,948.00)	(784.00)	(1,320.00)	(856.00)	(2,247.80)	(2,133.35)	(1,191.11)	2,424.50	1,888.50	2,352.50

Fig 6.1.2 Contents of cashflow spreadsheet

Software Trainers Cashflow Forecast

Month:	Dec '87 Forecast	Jan '88 Forecast	Feb '88 Forecast	Mar '88 Forecast	Apr '88 Forecast	May '88 Forecast	Dec '87 Actual	Jan '88 Actual	Feb '88 Actual	Mar '88 Actual	Apr '88 Actual	May '88 Actual
RECEIPTS - General	3240	2000	2000	2000	2000	2000	1546.75+1163	2015.42	1885.49	3674.3	2000	2000
RECEIPTS Deposit A/C				360	360	360			1000	2000	360	360
RECEIPTS - Courses				1440	1440	1440			332.75	1444.31	1440	1440
TOTAL RECEIPTS	SUM(B8:B6)	SUM(C8:C6)	SUM(D8:D6)	SUM(E8:E6)	SUM(F8:F6)	SUM(G8:G6)	SUM(H8:H6)	SUM(I8:I6)	SUM(J8:J6)	SUM(K8:K6)	SUM(L8:L6)	SUM(M8:M6)
PAYMENTS												
Advertising	200	200	150	150	150	150	162.86	423.65	150	150	150	150
Stationery	65	65	50	50	50	50		65	50	50	50	50
To creditors	65	65	65	65	65	65	65	65	65	65	65	65
Wages & Salaries	200	200	200	200	200	200	202	200	200	200	200	200
Rent/Rates		160			400			257.94			400	
Electricity	25	25	25	25	25	25	0	10.24	25	25	25	25
Transport - Car	96	96	96	96	96	96	96	96	96	96	96	96
Transport - Petrol	80	80	80	80	80	80	119.66	95.36	80	80	80	80
Equipment Leasing	100	100	100	100	460	460	100	100	100	556	460	460
Telephone	40	40	40	40	40	40	193.59	52.33	40	311	40	40
Postage	20	20	20	20	20	20	1.24+2.6+1.8	9.72	20	20	20	20
VAT	400				600			578.03			600	
Drawings	1400	1400	1400	1400	2100	2100	2800	0	1400	1900	2100	2100
Petty Cash	50	50	50	50	50	50	.24+8.61+6.5	12.7	50	50	50	50
TOTAL EXPENSES	SUM(B12:B25)	SUM(C12:C25)	SUM(D12:D25)	SUM(E12:E25)	SUM(F12:F25)	SUM(G12:G25)	SUM(H12:H25)	SUM(I12:I25)	SUM(J12:J25)	SUM(K12:K25)	SUM(L12:L25)	SUM(M12:M25)
NET	B9-B27	C9-C27	D9-D27	E9-E27	F9-F27	G9-G27	H9-H27	I9-I27	J9-J27	K9-K27	L9-L27	M9-M27
Balance from previous month	-1800	B32	C32	D32	E32	F32	B31	H32	I32	J32	K32	L32
Net balance	B29+B31	C29+C31	D29+D31	E29+E31	F29+F31	G29+G31	H29+H31	I29+I31	J29+J31	K29+K31	L29+L31	M29+M31

Fig 6.1.3 *Graph drawn from cashflow spreadsheet*

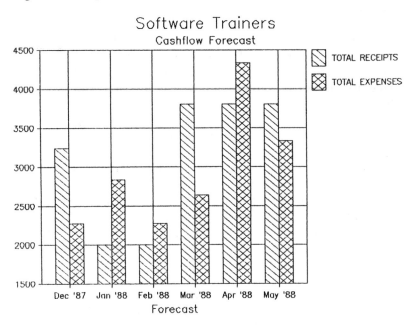

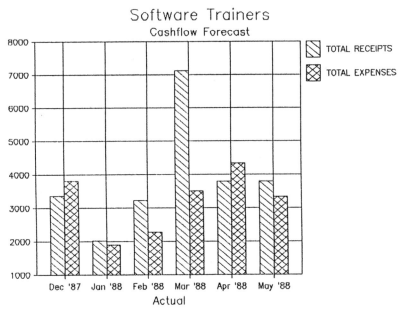

6.2 A PRICE LIST

The next example is a price list of goods whose prices in various foreign currencies need to be recalculated each time the rate of exchange alters. The rates of exchange are displayed at the top of the sheet and the price list itself is shown below. To do this you must be able to:

1. Change the widths of columns to accommodate large figures
2. Format certain columns for currencies that include small denominations of coins (as in dollars and cents) and for currencies where such subdivisions are not needed as with Italian Lire
3. Replicate a calculation keeping one entry constant.
4. Produce continuous lines across the sheet, both double and single

The display of the worksheet is shown in Figure 6.2.1 and the contents of the cells is shown in Figure 6.2.2.

This example was produced using SuperCalc.

Fig 6.2.1 *Price list spreadsheet*

	A	B	C	D	E	F	G	H
1	RATES OF EXCHANGE							
2	---							
3	USA	1.66	Dollars					
4	France	9.95	Francs					
5	Germany	3.21	Marks					
6	Italy	2,012.00	Lire					
7	Greece	212.00	Drachma					
8	Belgium	602.00	Francs					
9	===							
10	PRICE LIST							
11	---							
12	Cat.No.	Price - #	Price - $	Price - FF	Price - DM	Price - L	Price - Dr	Price - BF
13	---							
14	09-123	23.78	39.47	236.61	76.33	47845	5041	14316
15	09-125	26.97	44.77	268.35	86.57	54264	5718	16236
16	09-132	27.98	46.45	278.40	89.82	56296	5932	16844
17	09-143	30.55	50.71	303.97	98.07	61467	6477	18391
18	10-123	56.71	94.14	564.26	182.04	114101	12023	34139
19	10-125	58.88	97.74	585.86	189.00	118467	12483	35446
20	10-132	60.78	100.89	604.76	195.10	122289	12885	36590
21	10-142	62.12	103.12	618.09	199.41	124985	13169	37396

Fig 6.2.2 *Contents of price list spreadsheet*

	A	B	C	D	E	F	G	H
1	RATES OF EXCHANGE							
2	---							
3	USA	1.66	Dollars					
4	France	9.95	Francs					
5	Germany	3.21	Marks					
6	Italy	2012	Lire					
7	Greece	212	Drachma					
8	Belgium	602	Francs					
9	===							
10	PRICE LIST							
11	---							
12	Cat.No.	Price - #	Price - $	Price - FF	Price - DM	Price - L	Price - Dr	Price - BF
13	---							
14	09-123	23.78	+B14*B3	+B14*B4	+B14*B5	+B14*B6	+B14*B7	+B14*B8
15	09-125	26.97	+B15*B3	+B15*B4	+B15*B5	+B15*B6	+B15*B7	+B15*B8
16	09-132	27.98	+B16*B3	+B16*B4	+B16*B5	+B16*B6	+B16*B7	+B16*B8
17	09-143	30.55	+B17*B3	+B17*B4	+B17*B5	+B17*B6	+B17*B7	+B17*B8
18	10-123	56.71	+B18*B3	+B18*B4	+B18*B5	+B18*B6	+B18*B7	+B18*B8
19	10-125	58.88	+B19*B3	+B19*B4	+B19*B5	+B19*B6	+B19*B7	+B19*B8
20	10-132	60.78	+B20*B3	+B20*B4	+B20*B5	+B20*B6	+B20*B7	+B20*B8
21	10-142	62.12	+B21*B3	+B21*B4	+B21*B5	+B21*B6	+B21*B7	+B21*B8

6.3 STOCK RECORDS

In this example part of the stock record for a wholesale electrical company is shown. From this you can discover what items need re-ordering, when the number in stock is below the re-order level. This entails using the worksheet as a database. In order to do this you need to be able to:

1. Define the data range covering the items
2. Define the criterion range where the test is entered
3. Define the output range where the results of the selection will be displayed
4. Enter a criterion (D2<E2)
5. Calculate the VAT by multiplying the contents of column G by .15
6. Calculate the total price by adding the contents of columns H and G and displaying in column I
7. Format columns to display in pounds and pence

The result of the test is shown in the display of the whole worksheet in Figure 6.3.1

The second figure, Figure 6.3.2 shows the sheet modified to display the total value of the stock. In order to do this you need to be able to:

1. Insert an extra column I
2. Calculate the individual stock values by multiplying the contents of column D by the contents of column F and placing the answer in a new column I
3. Hide the contents of the new column so that they are not displayed by reducing the width of the column to zero
4. Use the **sum** function to add a series of entries together (SUM(I2:I22))

This worksheet was prepared using SuperCalc4.

Fig 6.3.1 *Stock record spreadsheet*

	A	B	C	D	E	F	G	H	I	J
1	Stock No	Description	Pk Qty	In Stock	Reorder Level	Cost Price	Selling price	VAT @ 15%	Total Price	
2	4013	Fuse - 50 mA	10	345	200	3.67	5.19	.78	5.97	
3	4014	Fuse - 63 mA	10	321	200	3.67	5.19	.78	5.97	
4	4015	Fuse - 80 mA	10	66	100	1.25	5.19	.78	5.97	
5	4016	Fuse - 100 mA	10	90	85	1.25	.53	.08	.61	
6	4017	Fuse - 125 mA	10	78	100	1.25	.53	.08	.61	
7	4018	Fuse - 160 mA	10	32	50	1.25	.53	.08	.61	
8	4019	Fuse - 200 mA	10	239	150	1.25	.53	.08	.61	
9	4020	Fuse - 250 mA	10	125	100	.98	1.52	.23	1.75	
10	4021	Fuse - 300 mA	10	76	100	.98	1.52	.23	1.75	
11	4022	Fuse - 315 mA	10	54	50	.98	1.52	.23	1.75	
12	4023	Fuse - 400 mA	10	98	100	.98	1.52	.23	1.75	
13	4024	Fuse - 500 mA	10	344	200	.98	1.52	.23	1.75	
14	4025	Fuse - 600 mA	10	129	100	.98	1.52	.23	1.75	
15	4026	Fuse - 630 mA	10	200	200	.98	1.52	.23	1.75	
16	4027	Fuse - 800 mA	10	321	100	.98	1.52	.23	1.75	
17	4028	Fuse - 1A	10	31	50	.98	1.52	.23	1.75	
18	4029	Fuse - 1.25A	10	43	50	.98	1.52	.23	1.75	
19	4030	Fuse - 1.6A	10	86	50	.98	1.52	.23	1.75	
20	4031	Fuse - 2A	10	65	50	.98	1.52	.23	1.75	
21	4032	Fuse - 2.5A	10	54	50	1.60	2.22	.33	2.55	
22	4033	Fuse - 3.15A	10	34	50	1.60	2.22	.33	2.55	
23										
24	In Stock									
25	0									
26										
27										
28	To be reordered									
29	==================									
30	Stock No	Description								
31	4015	Fuse - 80 mA								
32	4017	Fuse - 125 mA								
33	4018	Fuse - 160 mA								
34	4021	Fuse - 300 mA								
35	4023	Fuse - 400 mA								
36	4028	Fuse - 1A								
37	4029	Fuse - 1.25A								
38	4033	Fuse - 3.15A								
39										
40										
41										
42										

112

Fig 6.3.2 *Stock valuation spreadsheet*

```
41
42
```

	A	B	C	D	E	F	G	H	J	K
1	Stock No Description	Pk Qty	In Stock	Reorder Level	Cost Price	Selling price	VAT @ 15%	Total Price		
2	4013Fuse - 50 mA	10	345	200	3.67	5.19	.78	5.97		
3	4014Fuse - 63 mA	10	321	200	3.67	5.19	.78	5.97		
4	4015Fuse - 80 mA	10	66	100	1.25	5.19	.78	5.97		
5	4016Fuse - 100 mA	10	90	85	1.25	.53	.08	.61		
6	4017Fuse - 125 mA	10	78	100	1.25	.53	.08	.61		
7	4018Fuse - 160 mA	10	32	50	1.25	.53	.08	.61		
8	4019Fuse - 200 mA	10	239	150	1.25	.53	.08	.61		
9	4020Fuse - 250 mA	10	125	100	.98	1.52	.23	1.75		
10	4021Fuse - 300 mA	10	76	100	.98	1.52	.23	1.75		
11	4022Fuse - 315 mA	10	54	50	.98	1.52	.23	1.75		
12	4023Fuse - 400 mA	10	98	100	.98	1.52	.23	1.75		
13	4024Fuse - 500 mA	10	344	200	.98	1.52	.23	1.75		
14	4025Fuse - 600 mA	10	129	100	.98	1.52	.23	1.75		
15	4026Fuse - 630 mA	10	200	200	.98	1.52	.23	1.75		
16	4027Fuse - 800 mA	10	321	100	.98	1.52	.23	1.75		
17	4028Fuse - 1A	10	31	50	.98	1.52	.23	1.75		
18	4029Fuse - 1.25A	10	43	50	.98	1.52	.23	1.75		
19	4030Fuse - 1.6A	10	86	50	.98	1.52	.23	1.75		
20	4031Fuse - 2A	10	65	50	.98	1.52	.23	1.75		
21	4032Fuse - 2.5A	10	54	50	1.60	2.22	.33	2.55		
22	4033Fuse - 3.15A	10	34	50	1.60	2.22	.33	2.55		
23										
24	In Stock						Total value of stock	4756.83		
25	0									
26										
27										
28	To be reordered									
29	==================									
30	Stock No Description									
31	4015Fuse - 80 mA									
32	4017Fuse - 125 mA									
33	4018Fuse - 160 mA									
34	4021Fuse - 300 mA									
35	4023Fuse - 400 mA									
36	4028Fuse - 1A									
37	4029Fuse - 1.25A									
38	4033Fuse - 3.15A									
39										
40										
41										

6.4 LINKING SHEETS

The linking, or consolidation, of separate worksheets is an operation where you can amend a series of related worksheets individually and then take some or all of the information contained in them and write it on to a master worksheet. In order to do this you must be able to:

1. Create a series of worksheets, in identical formats if required
2. Create links between all or part of each of these sheets and one master sheet
3. Identify the source range of data on each sheet. Very often such ranges can be assigned names; this is technique is easier to apply than ranges given as cell references only
4. Update the sheets one after the other, probably using a macro file to do this
5. Consolidate the master sheet with information taken from the separate sheets, this information can either be added to existing data on the master sheet or overwrite existing information on this sheet
6. If you wish you can print out the final sheet or display it in the form of a graph, this is very easy to do if you use a macro to control the whole operation

An example is shown in the following illustrations. Figure 6.4.1 shows the empty master sheet. Figures 6.4.2 and 6.4.3 show two of the separate sheets and Figure 6.4.4 shows the master sheet after the sheets have been consolidated on to it.

114

Fig 6.4.1 *Empty master sheet*

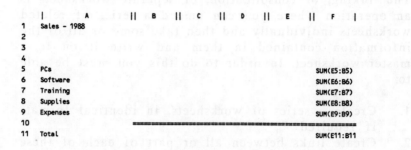

	A		B		C		D		E		F	
1	Sales - 1988											
2												
3												
4												
5	PCs									SUM(E5:B5)		
6	Software									SUM(E6:B6)		
7	Training									SUM(E7:B7)		
8	Supplies									SUM(E8:B8)		
9	Expenses									SUM(E9:B9)		
10												
11	Total									SUM(E11:B11)		

Fig 6.4.2 *One separate sheet for consolidation*

	A		B	
1	Sales - 1988			
2				
3	Region		North East	
4				
5	PCs		54,000.00	
6	Software		2,500.00	
7	Training		2,000.00	
8	Supplies		2,300.00	
9	Expenses		1,212.00	
10			============	
11	Total		59,588.00	

Fig 6.4.3 *Another separate sheet for consolidation*

	A			B	
1	Sales - 1988				
2					
3	Region			South	
4					
5	PCs			65,430.00	
6	Software			2,165.00	
7	Training			1,250.00	
8	Supplies			5,001.00	
9	Expenses			1,567.00	
10				============	
11	Total			72,279.00	

Fig 6.4.4 *Master sheet after consolidation*

	A		B		C		D		E		F
1	Sales - 1988										
2											
3			North East		North West		South		West		
4											
5	PCs		54,000.00		52,100.00		65,430.00		43,210.00		214,740.00
6	Software		2,500.00		4,530.00		2,165.00		3,210.00		12,405.00
7	Training		2,000.00		3,210.00		1,250.00		3,210.00		9,670.00
8	Supplies		2,300.00		4,005.00		5,001.00		210.00		11,516.00
9	Expenses		1,212.00		565.00		1,567.00		2,170.00		5,514.00
10			==								
11	Total		59,588.00		63,280.00		72,279.00		47,670.00		242,817.00

6.5 INVOICES

An invoice containing details of the payments due for a number of transactions can be created on a spreadsheet by entering the raw details on to a ready prepared sheet so that the total and the VAT and carriage costs can be automatically calculated and the total of the bill printed at the bottom of the sheet. In order to do this you must be able to:

1. Have a pre-formatted blank invoice available on disk
2. Calculate VAT by adding 15% on to individual totals
3. Sum the costs and VAT
4. Add in the postage and packing using a lookup table if required
5. Handle the date and calculating 30-day discount if required
6. Protect part of the sheet (the headings and address of the company)
7. Print the invoice
8. Suppress the printing of zeroes

All the entries on the blank invoice form are protected and its contents are shown in Figure 6.5.1. All the entries for an order are made in rows 4 to 13 and are automatically copied into the invoice in rows 34 to 45. As the copying takes place the appropriate calculations are performed. The customer's address and delivery address are entered into the range D24:D31. A final completed invoice is shown in Figure 6.5.

Fig 6.5.1 *Contents of blank invoice form*

```
        |   A   || B ||    C     ||        D         ||  E   ||  F  ||  G  || H |
 1      ===============================================================================
 2             No. off      Width(mm)         Height(mm)      Price/sq.m Description Code
 3      ===============================================================================
 4       1
 5       2
 6       3
 7       4
 8       5
 9       6
10       7
11       8
12       9
13      10
14      ===============================================================================
15
16                           CLEERLITE GLASS COMPANY
17                           For all Glass and Glazing Requirements
18                           Unit 7, Saxon Road
19                           Eastwood
20                           NORFIELD NF3 7PR
21                           Tel: (09303) 260880      VAT No. 232 242 56
22      -------------------------------------------------------------------------------
23            Date:          Order No:
24      Delivery date:       Customer Address:
25                                           :
26                                           :
27                                           :
28                           Delivery Address:
29                                           :
30                                           :
31                                           :
32      -------------------------------------------------------------------------------
33      No. off    Width(mm)   Height(mm)   Area (sq.m)               Price/sq.m   Cost #   Description Code
34      B4         C4          D4           ROUND(A34*B34*C34/1000000,2)  E4        +E34+E34    F4
35      B5         C5          D5           ROUND(A35*B35*C35/1000000,2)  E5        +E35+E35    F5
36      B6         C6          D6           ROUND(A36*B36*C36/1000000,2)  E6        +E36+E36    F6
37      B7         C7          D7           ROUND(A37*B37*C37/1000000,2)  E7        +E37+E37    F7
38      B8         C8          D8           ROUND(A38*B38*C38/1000000,2)  E8        +E38+E38    F8
39      B9         C9          D9           ROUND(A39*B39*C39/1000000,2)  E9        +E39+E39    F9
40      B10        C10         D10          ROUND(A40*B40*C40/1000000,2)  E10       +E40+E40    F10
41      B11        C11         D11          ROUND(A41*B41*C41/1000000,2)  E11       +E41+E41    F11
42      B12        C12         D12          ROUND(A42*B42*C42/1000000,2)  E12       +E42+E42    F12
43      B13        C13         D13          ROUND(A43*B43*C43/1000000,2)  E13       +E43+E43    F13
44      -------------------------------------------------------------------------------
45                                              TOTAL  SUM(F43:F34)
46                                              VAT @ 15% F45*.15
47                                              Sub-Total +F46+F45
48
49
50                 If paid by : B24+30            5% discount is allowed
51
52
```

Fig 6.5.2 *Completed invoice*

CLEERLITE GLASS COMPANY
For all Glass and Glazing Requirements
Unit 7, Saxon Road
Eastwood
NORFIELD NF3 7PR
Tel: (09303)VAT No. 232 242 56

```
       Date: 1/12/88      Order No:     10102
Delivery date: 11/ 1/89 Customer Address:J.Walker
                                        :45 HomeGate
                                        :Winton
                                        :Swayford
                        Delivery Address:As above
                                        :
                                        :
                                        :
```

No. off	Width(mm)	Height(mm)	Area (sq.m)	Price/(sq.m)	Cost #	Description Code
3	3000	1000	9	7	43	1010
1	2500	1500	4	4	13	1011
2	500	750	1	3	9	9001

```
                              TOTAL      64.39
                              VAT @ 15%   9.66
                              Sub-Total  74.04


       If paid by : 10/ 2/1989  5% discount is allowed
```

6.6 DECISION MAKING

Spreadsheets provide us with facilities not only to perform complex arithmetic but also to make decisions automatically. This can be done by using functions that contain the keyword **IF** and those that enable us to link statements together in a logical manner using the standard logical operators **AND, OR** and **NOT**. There are also other logical functions that evaluate to **TRUE** (1) or **FALSE** (0).

The first example, written using the Multiplan spreadsheet program, shows the calculation of electricity bills where if the charge, assumed to be for three months, is less than $100 then this charge is divided by three and paid monthly instead. The test in column 4 decides if the charge is more than $100. If it is then the charge is divided by three. In the next column a similar test determines whether the word "monthly" should be displayed or not. Figure 6.6.1 shows the finished sheet and Figure 6.6.2 shows the contents of the cells. Multiplan uses numbers for both columns and rows so that **R1C7** means "**Row 1 Column 7**" and **RC[-1]** means "**the cell immediately to the left of this one**". Similarly, **RC[-2]** means "**the cell two columns to the left of this one**".

In the second example we have a club that offers discount to members depending on their age. If they are under 21 years old they get 5% discount on goods. Anyone over 21 years old gets 10% discount. If you are not a member of the club then you will get no discount unless you are over 75 years, when you get 7.5% discount. The test is shown in column 4. It becomes quite complicated until you realise that

NOT(RC[-2]=0

means "the contents of the cell in this row and two columns to the left is not equal to zero". Also the statement that

AND(RC[-1]>65,RC[-2]=0)

means "the contents of the cell in this row one column to the left is greater than 65 and the contents of the

cell in this row but two columns to the left equals zero".
The final sheet is shown in Figure 6.6.3 and the contents of the cells in Figure 6.6.4.
In order to produce this spreadsheet you must be able to:

1. Use the IF function in order to provide the program with two courses of action depending on the outcome of a test
2. Use the AND logical operator in conjunction with IF so that you will be able to decide the outcome of a test of the truth of two tests (if the two things connected by the "AND" are both true then the outcome is true, if one or both are not true then the result is false)
3. Use the NOT logical operator to negate the truth of a statement

NOTE: The **OR** logical operator works in a similar way to **AND** in that if either one of the tests is true then the result is true.

Fig 6.6.1   *The electricity bill spreadsheet*

				ELECTRICITY	Standing Charge	3.45
					Price per unit:	0.05
Customer Number	Present Reading	Previous Reading	Units Used	Charge		
3456	2345	1234	1111	59.00		
3245	6767	6500	267	16.80		
6789	3000	3000	0	3.45		
3215	2134	1678	456	26.25		
7689	7890	6900	990	52.95		
3216	4444	3432	1012	54.05		
5674	9078	3215	5863	98.87	Monthly	
6790	5000	4560	440	25.45		
4432	6543	4321	2222	38.18	Monthly	
1218	8001	7890	111	9.00		
5678	3428	2234	1194	63.15		
5439	768	0	768	41.85		
4567	1900	800	1100	58.45		
3218	2100	780	1320	69.45		
2222	5564	4356	1208	63.85		
		Total		680.75		
		Average				
		Bill:		45.38		

Fig 6.6.2 The contents of the electricity bill spreadsheet

	1	2	3	4	5	6	7
					"Standing Charge:"		3.45
					"Price per unit:"		0.05
1	"Customer"	"Present"	"ELECTRICITY BILLS"				
2	"Number"	"Reading"	"Previous"	"Units"	" Charge"		
3			"Reading"	"Used"			
4	REPT("-",64)	REPT("-",64)	REPT("-",64)	REPT("-",64)	REPT("-",64)		
5							
6	3456	2345	1234	+RC[-2]-RC[-1]	IF(R1C7+R2C7*RC[-1]>100,(R1C7+R2C7*RC[-1])/3,R1C7+R2C7*RC[-1])	IF(R1C7+R2C7*RC[-2]>100,"Monthly"," ")	
7	3245	6767	6500	+RC[-2]-RC[-1]	IF(R1C7+R2C7*RC[-1]>100,(R1C7+R2C7*RC[-1])/3,R1C7+R2C7*RC[-1])	IF(R1C7+R2C7*RC[-2]>100,"Monthly"," ")	
8	6789	3000	3000	+RC[-2]-RC[-1]	IF(R1C7+R2C7*RC[-1]>100,(R1C7+R2C7*RC[-1])/3,R1C7+R2C7*RC[-1])	IF(R1C7+R2C7*RC[-2]>100,"Monthly"," ")	
9	3215	2134	1678	+RC[-2]-RC[-1]	IF(R1C7+R2C7*RC[-1]>100,(R1C7+R2C7*RC[-1])/3,R1C7+R2C7*RC[-1])	IF(R1C7+R2C7*RC[-2]>100,"Monthly"," ")	
10	7689	7890	6900	+RC[-2]-RC[-1]	IF(R1C7+R2C7*RC[-1]>100,(R1C7+R2C7*RC[-1])/3,R1C7+R2C7*RC[-1])	IF(R1C7+R2C7*RC[-2]>100,"Monthly"," ")	
11	3216	4444	3432	+RC[-2]-RC[-1]	IF(R1C7+R2C7*RC[-1]>100,(R1C7+R2C7*RC[-1])/3,R1C7+R2C7*RC[-1])	IF(R1C7+R2C7*RC[-2]>100,"Monthly"," ")	
12	5674	9078	3215	+RC[-2]-RC[-1]	IF(R1C7+R2C7*RC[-1]>100,(R1C7+R2C7*RC[-1])/3,R1C7+R2C7*RC[-1])	IF(R1C7+R2C7*RC[-2]>100,"Monthly"," ")	
13	6790	5000	4560	+RC[-2]-RC[-1]	IF(R1C7+R2C7*RC[-1]>100,(R1C7+R2C7*RC[-1])/3,R1C7+R2C7*RC[-1])	IF(R1C7+R2C7*RC[-2]>100,"Monthly"," ")	
14	4432	6543	4321	+RC[-2]-RC[-1]	IF(R1C7+R2C7*RC[-1]>100,(R1C7+R2C7*RC[-1])/3,R1C7+R2C7*RC[-1])	IF(R1C7+R2C7*RC[-2]>100,"Monthly"," ")	
15	1218	8001	7890	+RC[-2]-RC[-1]	IF(R1C7+R2C7*RC[-1]>100,(R1C7+R2C7*RC[-1])/3,R1C7+R2C7*RC[-1])	IF(R1C7+R2C7*RC[-2]>100,"Monthly"," ")	
16	5678	3428	2234	+RC[-2]-RC[-1]	IF(R1C7+R2C7*RC[-1]>100,(R1C7+R2C7*RC[-1])/3,R1C7+R2C7*RC[-1])	IF(R1C7+R2C7*RC[-2]>100,"Monthly"," ")	
17	5439	768	0	+RC[-2]-RC[-1]	IF(R1C7+R2C7*RC[-1]>100,(R1C7+R2C7*RC[-1])/3,R1C7+R2C7*RC[-1])	IF(R1C7+R2C7*RC[-2]>100,"Monthly"," ")	
18	4567	1900	800	+RC[-2]-RC[-1]	IF(R1C7+R2C7*RC[-1]>100,(R1C7+R2C7*RC[-1])/3,R1C7+R2C7*RC[-1])	IF(R1C7+R2C7*RC[-2]>100,"Monthly"," ")	
19	3218	2100	780	+RC[-2]-RC[-1]	IF(R1C7+R2C7*RC[-1]>100,(R1C7+R2C7*RC[-1])/3,R1C7+R2C7*RC[-1])	IF(R1C7+R2C7*RC[-2]>100,"Monthly"," ")	
20	2222	5564	4356	+RC[-2]-RC[-1]	IF(R1C7+R2C7*RC[-1]>100,(R1C7+R2C7*RC[-1])/3,R1C7+R2C7*RC[-1])	IF(R1C7+R2C7*RC[-2]>100,"Monthly"," ")	
21				"Total"	SUM(R[-2]C:R[-16]C)		
22				"Average"	""		
23				"Bill:"	AVERAGE(R[-4]C:R[-18]C)		
24							

Fig 6.6.3 *The club spreadsheet*

Price	Member No	Age	Discount	Price paid
23.50	213	22	10.00%	21.15
21.45	0	77	7.50%	19.84
3.66	456	34	10.00%	3.29
4.99	0	33	0.00%	4.99
3.77	559	68	10.00%	3.39
12.89	111	34	10.00%	11.60
15.00	0	69	7.50%	13.88
45.99	886	69	10.00%	41.39
23.55	342	18	5.00%	22.37
2.00	190	21	5.00%	1.90

Fig 6.6.4 *The contents of the club spreadsheet*

	1	2	3	4	5
1	"Price"	"Member No"	"Age"	"Discount"	"Price paid"
2	REPT("-",64)	REPT("-",64)	REPT("-",64)	REPT("-",64)	REPT("-",64)
3	23.5	213	22	IF(AND(RC[-1]>21,NOT(RC[-2]=0)),0.1,IF(AND(NOT(RC[-2]=0),NOT(RC[-1]>21)),0.05,IF(AND(RC[-1]>65 ,RC[-2]=0),0.075,0)))	RC[-4]*(1-RC[-1])
4	21.45	0	77	IF(AND(RC[-1]>21,NOT(RC[-2]=0)),0.1,IF(AND(NOT(RC[-2]=0),NOT(RC[-1]>21)),0.05,IF(AND(RC[-1]>65 ,RC[-2]=0),0.075,0)))	RC[-4]*(1-RC[-1])
5	3.66	456	34	IF(AND(RC[-1]>21,NOT(RC[-2]=0)),0.1,IF(AND(NOT(RC[-2]=0),NOT(RC[-1]>21)),0.05,IF(AND(RC[-1]>65 ,RC[-2]=0),0.075,0)))	RC[-4]*(1-RC[-1])
6	4.99	0	33	IF(AND(RC[-1]>21,NOT(RC[-2]=0)),0.1,IF(AND(NOT(RC[-2]=0),NOT(RC[-1]>21)),0.05,IF(AND(RC[-1]>65 ,RC[-2]=0),0.075,0)))	RC[-4]*(1-RC[-1])
7	3.77	559	68	IF(AND(RC[-1]>21,NOT(RC[-2]=0)),0.1,IF(AND(NOT(RC[-2]=0),NOT(RC[-1]>21)),0.05,IF(AND(RC[-1]>65 ,RC[-2]=0),0.075,0)))	RC[-4]*(1-RC[-1])
8	12.89	111	34	IF(AND(RC[-1]>21,NOT(RC[-2]=0)),0.1,IF(AND(NOT(RC[-2]=0),NOT(RC[-1]>21)),0.05,IF(AND(RC[-1]>65 ,RC[-2]=0),0.075,0)))	RC[-4]*(1-RC[-1])
9	15	0	69	IF(AND(RC[-1]>21,NOT(RC[-2]=0)),0.1,IF(AND(NOT(RC[-2]=0),NOT(RC[-1]>21)),0.05,IF(AND(RC[-1]>65 ,RC[-2]=0),0.075,0)))	RC[-4]*(1-RC[-1])
10	45.99	886	69	IF(AND(RC[-1]>21,NOT(RC[-2]=0)),0.1,IF(AND(NOT(RC[-2]=0),NOT(RC[-1]>21)),0.05,IF(AND(RC[-1]>65 ,RC[-2]=0),0.075,0)))	RC[-4]*(1-RC[-1])
11	23.55	342	18	IF(AND(RC[-1]>21,NOT(RC[-2]=0)),0.1,IF(AND(NOT(RC[-2]=0),NOT(RC[-1]>21)),0.05,IF(AND(RC[-1]>65 ,RC[-2]=0),0.075,0)))	RC[-4]*(1-RC[-1])
12	2	190	21	IF(AND(RC[-1]>21,NOT(RC[-2]=0)),0.1,IF(AND(NOT(RC[-2]=0),NOT(RC[-1]>21)),0.05,IF(AND(RC[-1]>65 ,RC[-2]=0),0.075,0)))	RC[-4]*(1-RC[-1])

6.7 STATISTICS

Spreadsheet programs offer considerable scope for statistical analysis. A lot of the effort is taken out of routine statistical calculations by the use of such things as averages, square roots, standard deviation and variance being available as common spreadsheet functions.
The first example shows regression analysis as offered by Lotus 1-2-3. This is a feature that comes as a standard procedure chosen from the main menu of Lotus commands. The example commences with a simple spreadsheet as shown in Figure 6.7.1. It shows the change in the cost of production per unit as the numbers, of cat-flaps in this case, increase from 40 to 1500.

Fig 6.7.1 *Basic spreadsheet of production costs*

Production	Unit cost
100	40
150	37
340	25
400	20
800	15
1000	10
1250	9
1500	4

By choosing regression analysis from the Lotus menu and telling it to "Go" the sheet, without any further entries from you, becomes as shown in Figure 6.7.2. Using the information produced by the regression analysis the line of best fit is obtained from the **Constant** and the **X coefficient** figures displayed at the bottom of the sheet. These two figures are then used to produce the third column at the top (shown in Figure 6.7.3). From these figures a graph can be drawn and this is shown in Figure 6.7.4.

Fig 6.7.2 *Regression calculation completed*

```
Production  Unit cost

    100         40
    150         37
    340         25
    400         20
    800         15
   1000         10
   1250          9
   1500          4
```

```
           Regression Output:
Constant                      36.37541
Std Err of Y Est               4.831672
R Squared                      0.884810
No. of Observations                   8
Degrees of Freedom                    6

X Coefficient(s)       -0.02364
```

Fig 6.7.3 *Line of best fit calculated*

```
Production  Unit cost  Line of best fit

    100        40 34.01073
    150        37 32.82839
    340        25 28.33549
    400        20 26.91669
    800        15 17.45796
   1000        10 12.72860
   1250         9 6.816906
   1500         4 0.905204
```

```
           Regression Output:
Constant                      36.37541
Std Err of Y Est               4.831672
R Squared                      0.884810
No. of Observations                   8
Degrees of Freedom                    6

X Coefficient(s)       -0.02364
```

Fig 6.7.4 *Graph of production costs plotted*

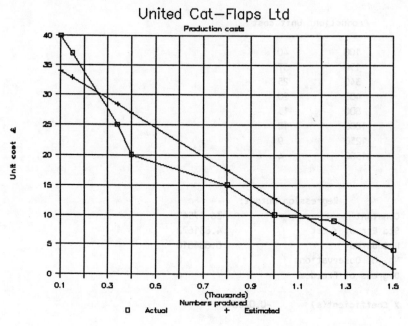

In order to produce this spreadsheet you must be able to:

1. Produce two data columns ready for production of an X-Y graph
2. Use the regression calculation feature of Lotus 1-2-3
3. Use the data from the regression calculation to produce a regression line
4. Plot two X-Y graphs on the same grid
5. Title and label the graph details

The next example shows the use of the **STD**, **AVG** and **SQRT** functions. It also shows how we can generate random numbers. The spreadsheet used here was SuperCalc and its random number function is called **RND()**. Figure 6.7.5 shows the contents of the sheet where the average of the figures in column A is calculated in cell A20. Then the table of the difference between each number and this average (the deviation of each number from the average) is calculated in column B. Column C contains the square of each of the deviations. Then in cells C20 and D20 the average of the squares of the deviations is calculated together with the square root of this figure. To show the accuracy of the **STD** function this calculates the standard deviation in cell E20 and as you would expect, the two answers are the same as you see in Figure 6.7.6.

Fig 6.7.5 *Contents of standard deviation spreadsheet*

	A		B		C		D		E		F		G	
1	RAN()	+A1-A2 B1^2				
2	RAN()	+A2-A2 B2^2				
3	RAN()	+A3-A2 B3^2				
4	RAN()	+A4-A2 B4^2				
5	RAN()	+A5-A2 B5^2				
6	RAN()	+A6-A2 B6^2				
7	RAN()	+A7-A2 B7^2				
8	RAN()	+A8-A2 B8^2				
9	RAN()	+A9-A2 B9^2				
10	RAN()	+A10-A B10^2				
11	RAN()	+A11-A B11^2				
12	RAN()	+A12-A B12^2				
13	RAN()	+A13-A B13^2				
14	RAN()	+A14-A B14^2				
15	RAN()	+A15-A B15^2				
16	RAN()	+A16-A B16^2				
17	RAN()	+A17-A B17^2				
18	RAN()	+A18-A B18^2				
19	---------	------------				
20	AVG(A18:A1)	AVG(C18:C1) SQRT(C20)		STD(A1:A18)		

Fig 6.7.6 *Standard deviation spreadsheet*

	A		B		C		D		E		F		G	
1	.5808205	.1459214	.0212930584			
2	.6025614	.1676623	.0281106544			
3	.3201753	-.114724	.0131615566			
4	.0219065	-.412993	.1705628770			
5	.7383116	.3034125	.0920591335			
6	.2889450	-.145954	.0213025804			
7	.1181306	-.316769	.1003423010			
8	.7663188	.3314197	.1098390482			
9	.7898532	.3549542	.1259924562			
10	.7316550	.2967560	.0880640962			
11	.4568792	.0219801	.0004831259			
12	.1099005	-.324999	.1056241018			
13	.7375577	.3026586	.0916022289			
14	.1947101	-.240189	.0576907400			
15	.3387640	-.096135	.0092419476			
16	.3455039	-.089395	.0079915008			
17	.1879856	-.246913	.0609662485			
18	.4982045	.0633054	.0040075800			
19	---------		------------			
20	.4348991		.0615741797 .2481415		.2481415		

To produce this spreadsheet you must be able to:

1. Use the random number generator function
2. Use the AVG, SQRT and STD functions

6.8 MATHEMATICS

Spreadsheets can be of great use not only in the world of finance and business but also in the solution of mathematics problems at many levels. This means that they can be of great value in Education. The teacher who has to produce a large number of problems of the same type can be saved the labour of repetitious calculation by setting up a spreadsheet to solve a general problem and then using the "What-if" approach. By keying in the appropriate numbers the solutions will be easily obtained in a fraction of the usual time. Another great benefit of the use of spreadsheet programs in the teaching of mathematics is that it becomes very simple to demonstrate many mathematical techniques in a very clear and easily understandable manner. For example, the demonstration of the convergence of series can be undertaken by using a technique involving circular references. A circular reference is one where a cell either directly or indirectly refers to itself. Two examples of this are shown first. One deals with the examination of convergent series and the other with the solution of equations by the method of "iteration". Figure 6.8.1 shows a spreadsheet set up to find the sum of the series

$$1/1 + 1/2 + 1/3 + 1/4 + 1/5 + \ldots$$

Fig 6.8.1 *Contents of spreadsheet to compute sum of a series*

```
            A       B       C       D       E       F       G       H
 1  +a1+1
 2  +IF(INT(a1/2)=a1/2,1/a1,-1/a1)
 3  +a3+a2
 4
 5
 6
 7
 8
 9
10
11
12
13
14
15
16
17
18
19
20
0% USED 10:21 am  A1(EXPR)=a1+1
ENTER: Use arrow keys to move around, HELP(F1), or one of the following:
  +Expr "Text 'Rpt ,Graph <Time /Cmd =Goto !Recalc ;Jump
```

Note the circular reference in cell A1. Whenever the
Recalculation key is pressed the number displayed in
this cell is increased by one. This number is tested in
cell A2 and the next number to be added to the series is
made either positive or negative according to whether
the number in A1 is odd or even. The amount by which the
sum is increased is displayed in this cell. The sum of
the terms is accumulated in cell A3 - another circular
reference. Figure 6.8.2 shows the display after fifty
calculations have been made.

Fig 6.8.2 *Series computation after 50 calculations*

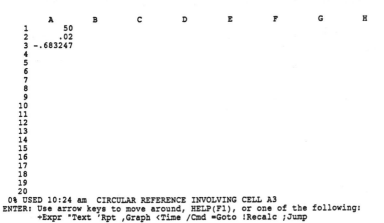

```
       A      B     C     D     E     F     G     H
 1       50
 2      .02
 3  -.683247
 4
 5
 6
 7
 8
 9
10
11
12
13
14
15
16
17
18
19
20
0% USED 10:24 am   CIRCULAR REFERENCE INVOLVING CELL A3
ENTER: Use arrow keys to move around, HELP(F1), or one of the following:
       +Expr "Text 'Rpt ,Graph <Time /Cmd =Goto !Recalc ;Jump
```

The solution of pairs of simultaneous equations can be
solved using a similar kind of method. In this case the
technique of *iteration* is being used. The method, of
course, can be extended to cover the solution of any
number of simultaneous equations.

The equations being solved in this example are:

$$3X + 2Y = 0$$
$$X + Y = -1$$

and for the purpose of this method they are re-written
so that one gives Y in terms of X and the other gives X
in terms of Y:

$$X = -2Y/3$$

$$Y = -X - 1$$

The basic spreadsheet looks as shown in Figure 6.8.3, where the coefficients of the original equations are in cells A1 to C1 and A2 to C2. The re-written equations are in cells B3 and B4. As the calculation has not started at this point the numbers 0 and -1 are displayed in these two cells. Then the recalculation key is pressed. After five recalculations the sheet looks as shown in Figure 6.8.4 and after forty recalculations it has reached the answer as displayed in Figure 6.8.5.

Fig 6.8.3 *Spreadsheet for solution of simultaneous equations by iteration*

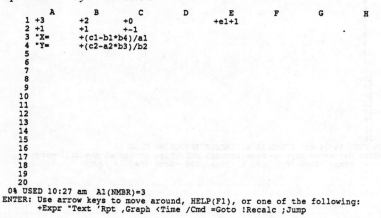

Fig 6.8.4 *Solution of simultaneous equations after five iterations*

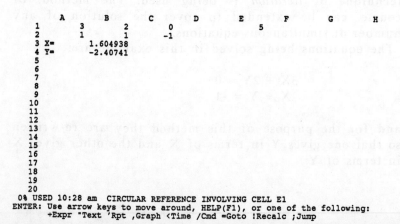

Fig 6.8.5 *Solution of simultaneous equations after forty iterations*

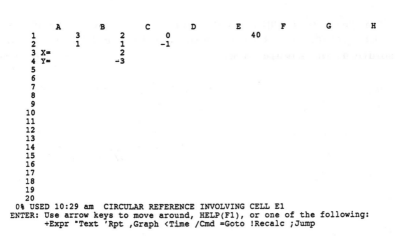

```
       A      B      C      D      E      F      G      H
 1      3      2      0            40
 2      1      1     -1
 3 X=          2
 4 Y=         -3
 5
 6
 7
 8
 9
10
11
12
13
14
15
16
17
18
19
20
0% USED 10:29 am  CIRCULAR REFERENCE INVOLVING CELL E1
ENTER: Use arrow keys to move around, HELP(F1), or one of the following:
 +Expr "Text 'Rpt ,Graph <Time /Cmd =Goto !Recalc ;Jump
```

In order to produce these spreadsheets you must be able to:

1. Use a circular reference method
2. Force recalculation to take place only when the RECALC key is pressed (you may have to select **Manual Recalculation** before you do this otherwise the calculation may run away with you)

If you wish you can solve simultaneous equations more directly by using a general formula. This entails writing a pair of equations in general terms first and then producing a formula for the general solution for both X and Y:

$$a_1 X + b_1 Y = c_1$$

$$a_2 X + b_2 Y = c_2$$

produces the formulas

130

$$X = (a_1c_2 - a_2c_1)/(a_1b_2 - a_2b_1)$$

$$Y = (c_1b_2 - c_2b_1)/(a_1b_2 - a_2b_1)$$

This pair of formulas can then be used as a basis for your spreadsheet. This is shown in Figure 6.8.6 with the solution in Figure 6.8.7.

Fig 6.8.6 *Solution of simultaneous equations by formula*

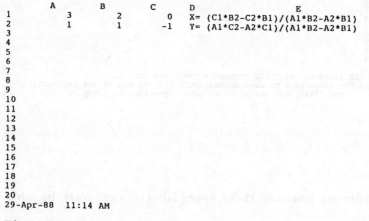

```
E1: (T) [W34] (C1*B2-C2*B1)/(A1*B2-A2*B1)

      A        B        C     D              E
1         3        2        0   X=  (C1*B2-C2*B1)/(A1*B2-A2*B1)
2         1        1       -1   Y=  (A1*C2-A2*C1)/(A1*B2-A2*B1)
3
4
5
6
7
8
9
10
11
12
13
14
15
16
17
18
19
20
29-Apr-88   11:14 AM
```

Fig 6.8.7 *Solution of simultaneous equations displayed*

```
E2: (G) [W5] (A1*C2-A2*C1)/(A1*B2-A2*B1)

      A        B        C     D     E     F     G     H
1         3        2        0   X=    2
2         1        1       -1   Y=   -3
3
4
5
6
7
8
9
10
11
12
13
14
15
16
17
18
19
20
29-Apr-88   11:15 AM
```

In order to produce this spreadsheet you must be able to:

1. Rearrange the equations to provide two formulas in terms of the coefficients only

A feature not readily available in all spreadsheet programs is that of matrix manipulation. Lotus 1-2-3, however, provides this. It allows you to invert and multiply matrices with great ease. The spreadsheet shown in Figure 6.8.8 shows the display for the solution of the pair of equations

$$3X + 2Y = 0$$
$$X + Y = -1$$

already solved by two different methods earlier. The coefficients are in cells A1 to C1 and A2 to C2. You can now ask for the program to invert the matrix of numbers in the block of cells A1:B2. The result of the inversion is displayed in the block A4:C5. This inverted matrix is then multiplied by the column matrix in C1:C2 with the final result displayed in C4:C5. We now have the solution to the equations displayed.

Fig 6.8.8 *Solution of equations using matrix inversion and multiplication*

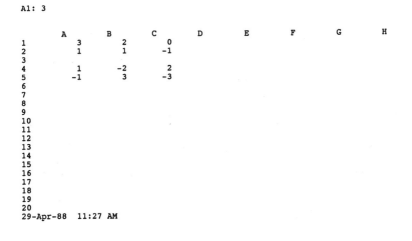

```
A1: 3

         A        B        C        D        E        F        G        H
1        3        2        0
2        1        1       -1
3
4        1       -2        2
5       -1        3       -3
6
7
8
9
10
11
12
13
14
15
16
17
18
19
20
29-Apr-88  11:27 AM
```

In order to produce this spreadsheet you must be able to:

1. Use the matrix inversion and multiplication routines offered by Lotus 1-2-3
2. Create formulas for the multiplication and inversion of matrices if such routines do not exist in your spreadsheet program

EXTRAS

7.1 PRINTING SIDEWAYS

It is not uncommon for us to have a spreadsheet that is very wide and cannot be printed in its entirety across one sheet of paper. Although you can arrange for your printout to be in compressed print rather than ordinary sized print it is still not always possible to get away from the tyranny of sticky tape and several sheets of paper. If you want to arrange for compressed print you can deal with this by sending a *set-up code* to your printer to tell it to print in small characters rather than large ones. Examples of normal-sized print and compressed print are shown in Figures 7.1 and 7.2.

Fig 7.1 *Spreadsheet in normal-sized characters*

Rank	Company	Sales '000s Current Year	Sales '000s Previous Year	Change %
1	British Petroleum	40,986,000	37,933,000	8.0%
2	Shell Transport & Trading	25,237,600	25,417,000	-0.7%
3	Unilever	16,693,000	16,172,000	3.2%
4	Electricity Council	10,742,600	9,941,500	8.1%
5	ICI	10,725,000	9,909,000	8.2%
6	BAT Industries	8,797,000	10,079,000	-12.7%
7	Esso UK	8,500,700	6,232,900	36.4%
8	British Telecom	8,387,000	7,653,000	9.6%
9	British Gas	7,687,200	6,913,500	11.2%
10	S & W Berisford	7,291,827	5,703,000	27.9%
11	Shell UK	7,215,000	8,098,000	-10.9%
12	Grand Metropolitan	5,589,500	5,075,000	10.1%
13	RTZ Corporation	5,310,800	5,948,600	-10.7%
14	General Electric Company	5,253,000	5,222,000	0.6%
15	British National Oil Corp	4,928,075	9,561,957	-48.5%
16	Imperial Group	4,918,600	4,593,000	7.1%
17	Phibro UK	4,896,600	4,764,000	2.8%
18	Ford Motor Company	4,045,000	3,752,000	7.8%
19	BTR	3,880,600	3,486,700	11.3%
20	Dalgety	3,767,000	3,701,000	1.8%

Fig 7.2 *Spreadsheet in compressed print*

Rank	Company	Sales £'000s Current Year	Sales £'000s Previous Year	Change %	Pre-Tax Profits £'000s	Rank	Pre-Tax Profit as % of Sales	Rank
1	British Petroleum	40,986,000	37,933,000	8.0%	3,613,000	1	8.8%	10
2	Shell Transport & Trading	25,237,600	25,417,000	-0.7%	3,208,000	2	12.7%	7
3	Unilever	16,693,000	16,172,000	3.2%	978,000	7	5.9%	14
4	Electricity Council	10,742,600	9,941,500	8.1%	944,200	8	8.8%	11
5	ICI	10,725,000	9,909,000	8.2%	904,000	9	8.4%	12
6	BAT Industries	8,797,000	10,079,000	-12.7%	1,168,000	6	13.3%	6
7	Esso UK	8,500,700	6,232,900	36.4%	1,272,000	5	15.0%	3
8	British Telecom	8,387,000	7,653,000	9.6%	1,810,000	4	21.6%	2
9	British Gas	7,687,200	6,913,500	11.2%	687,800	12	8.9%	9
10	S & W Berisford	7,291,827	5,703,000	27.9%	52,951	18	0.7%	18
11	Shell UK	7,215,000	8,098,000	-10.9%	2,120,000	3	29.4%	1
12	Grand Metropolitan	5,589,500	5,075,000	10.1%	347,300	14	6.2%	13
13	RTZ Corporation	5,310,800	5,948,600	-10.7%	713,900	10	13.4%	4
14	General Electric Company	5,253,000	5,222,000	0.6%	701,000	11	13.3%	5
15	British National Oil Corp	4,928,075	9,561,957	-48.5%	13,310	19	0.3%	19
16	Imperial Group	4,918,600	4,593,000	7.1%	235,700	15	4.8%	15
17	Phibro UK	4,896,600	4,764,000	2.8%	12,600	20	0.3%	20
18	Ford Motor Company	4,045,000	3,752,000	7.8%	160,000	16	4.0%	16
19	BTR	3,880,600	3,486,700	11.3%	361,800	13	9.3%	8
20	Dalgety	3,767,000	3,701,000	1.8%	65,800	17	1.7%	17

Certain spreadsheets are able to accept additional code strings that will compress the print even more, as is shown in Figure 7.3, but the real answer to the problem is to use a program that will print the sheet along the length of the printer paper rather than across it.

Fig 7.3 *Further compressed print on a spreadsheet*

There are times, however, when your spreadsheet is too wide even for these methods to produce what you want. Then the time has come for you to use one of the pieces of software that will allow your spreadsheet to be printed sideways. By printing sideways, that is at right angles to the usual direction of printing, you will be able to accommodate very wide sheets, as shown in Figure 7.4. There is a program called SIDEWAYS that will take a spreadsheet that has been saved to disk in "print" format (that is with a .PRN extension). This program will then take this file and print it as required. Certain spreadsheet programs, LOGISTIX being one, have a ready built-in function that will perform this operation by giving you the option, when it comes to printing your spreadsheet, of horizontal or vertical printing.

Fig 7.4 *The spreadsheet printed using the SIDEWAYS program*

Rank	Company		Rank	No. of Employees
1	British Petroleum		6	129,450
2	Shell Transport & Trading		14	312,000
3	Unilever		10	132,858
4	Electricity Council		8	118,600
5	ICI		15	185,503
6	BAT Industries		3	6,097
7	Esso UK		18	233,711
8	British Telecom		9	91,876
9	British Gas		4	10,871
10	S & W Berisford		5	15,558
11	Shell UK		17	137,195
12	Grand Metropolitan		12	75,197
13	RTZ Corporation		19	165,593
14	General Electric Company		1	86
15	British National Oil Corp		13	89,014
16	Imperial Group		2	628
17	Phibro UK		11	53,300
18	Ford Motor Company		16	85,400
19	BTR		7	18,951
20	Dalgety			

7.2 USING LOTUS HAL

Apart from programs such as SIDEWAYS, described in section 7.1, there are other "add-on" programs available that make the use of spreadsheets even easier. One of these is the Lotus product called HAL. This enables you to issue spreadsheet commands to Lotus 1-2-3 in English rather than in a series of command letters. When the HAL program is installed the HAL prompt is invoked by pressing the \ key. The word REQUEST appears in the space where the usual Lotus commands are entered. This is shown in Figure 7.5. The commands are then entered in what is almost a free English-style form. The first command is shown in the figure. Its effect is shown in Figure 7.6, which is quite dramatic the first time you see it! A new column is inserted at the current cursor position by the command shown in Figure 7.7 with its effect shown in Figure 7.8. Underlining the current row is effected by the single word "underline" with its effect shown in Figure 7.9. Figure 7.10 shows the command to enter days of the week in column A so that the result so far looks as shown in Figure 7.11. Figure 7.12 shows the command to leave HAL, the peremptory "go away". This leaves the sheet open for the entry of data as in Figure 7.13. By having the cursor in cell B9 and giving the command "total all cols", as in Figure 7.14, we get the result shown in Figure 7.15. A format command entered as in Figure 7.16 has the effect shown in Figure 7.17, but three columns have to be widened. This is done by the command shown in Figure 7.18 and 7.19.

Fig 7.5 *HAL request to enter month names across top of spreadsheet*

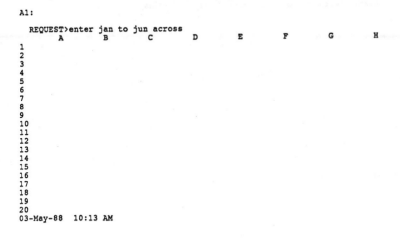

Fig 7.6 *Result of HAL request in Fig 7.5*

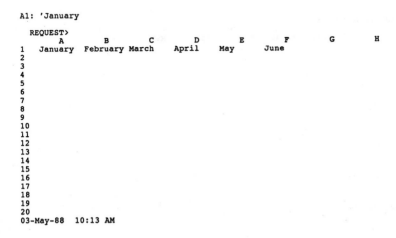

Fig 7.7 *HAL request to insert a new column*

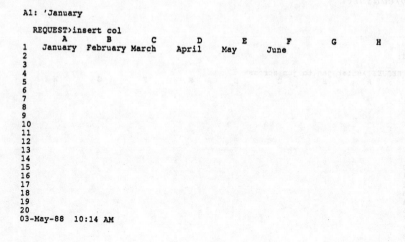

Fig 7.8 *HAL request to underline current row*

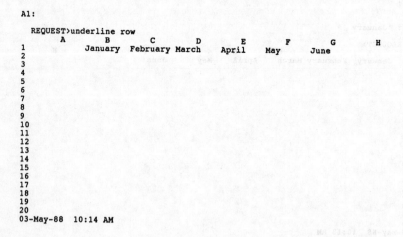

Fig 7.9 *Row underlined by HAL*

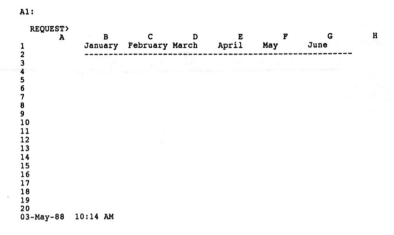

```
A1:
    REQUEST>
        A        B        C       D        E       F        G          H
    1           January February March   April    May     June
    2           ------------------------------------------------------
    3
    4
    5
    6
    7
    8
    9
   10
   11
   12
   13
   14
   15
   16
   17
   18
   19
   20
03-May-88   10:14 AM
```

Fig 7.10 *HAL request to enter days of the week in a column*

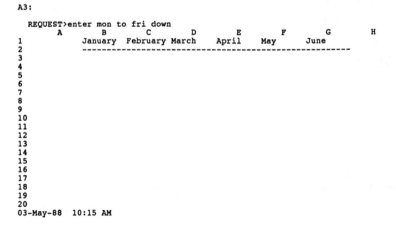

```
A3:
    REQUEST>enter mon to fri down
        A        B        C       D        E       F        G          H
    1           January February March   April    May     June
    2           ------------------------------------------------------
    3
    4
    5
    6
    7
    8
    9
   10
   11
   12
   13
   14
   15
   16
   17
   18
   19
   20
03-May-88   10:15 AM
```

Fig 7.11 *Result of HAL request shown in Fig 7.10*

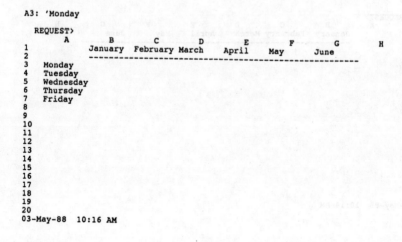

```
A3: 'Monday

   REQUEST>
       A       B         C        D       E       F       G       H
  1          January  February  March   April   May     June
  2          ----------------------------------------------------------
  3  Monday
  4  Tuesday
  5  Wednesday
  6  Thursday
  7  Friday
  8
  9
 10
 11
 12
 13
 14
 15
 16
 17
 18
 19
 20
03-May-88  10:16 AM
```

Fig 7.12 *Request to terminate HAL requests*

```
B3:

   REQUEST>go away
       A       B         C        D       E       F       G       H
  1          January  February  March   April   May     June
  2          ----------------------------------------------------------
  3  Monday
  4  Tuesday
  5  Wednesday
  6  Thursday
  7  Friday
  8
  9
 10
 11
 12
 13
 14
 15
 16
 17
 18
 19
 20
03-May-88  10:17 AM
```

Fig 7.13 *Sheet after data has been entered*

```
B9:

    REQUEST>
         A      B         C      D       E       F      G        H
    1        January February March   April   May     June
    2        ------------------------------------------------------------
    3  Monday      234      231    122     239     123    789
    4  Tuesday      34       43    189      32      89    678
    5  Wednesday    12       43     45      45      34    321
    6  Thursday    276       67     56      67     654    456
    7  Friday      238      179    678     345     789    459
    8        ------------------------------------------------------------
    9
   10
   11
   12
   13
   14
   15
   16
   17
   18
   19
   20
   03-May-88  10:19 AM
```

Fig 7.14 *HAL request to calculate totals*

```
B9:

    REQUEST>total all cols
         A      B         C      D       E       F      G        H
    1        January February March   April   May     June
    2        ------------------------------------------------------------
    3  Monday      234      231    122     239     123    789
    4  Tuesday      34       43    189      32      89    678
    5  Wednesday    12       43     45      45      34    321
    6  Thursday    276       67     56      67     654    456
    7  Friday      238      179    678     345     789    459
    8        ------------------------------------------------------------
    9
   10
   11
   12
   13
   14
   15
   16
   17
   18
   19
   20
   03-May-88  10:20 AM
```

142

Fig 7.15 *Result of request shown in Fig 7.14*

```
B9: @SUM(B3..B7)

   REQUEST>
      A        B        C        D        E        F        G        H
 1          January February March   April    May      June
 2          ----------------------------------------------------------------
 3  Monday      234      231      122      239      123      789
 4  Tuesday      34       43      189       32       89      678
 5  Wednesday    12       43       45       45       34      321
 6  Thursday    276       67       56       67      654      456
 7  Friday      238      179      678      345      789      459
 8          ----------------------------------------------------------------
 9              794      563 ·    1090      728     1689     2703
10
11
12
13
14
15
16
17
18
19
20
03-May-88  10:21 AM
```

Fig 7.16 *HAL format request*

```
B9: (G) @SUM(B3..B7)

   REQUEST>format this as $ with 2 decimals
      A        B        C        D        E        F        G        H
 1          January February March   April    May      June
 2          ----------------------------------------------------------------
 3  Monday      234      231      122      239      123      789
 4  Tuesday      34       43      189       32       89      678
 5  Wednesday    12       43       45       45       34      321
 6  Thursday    276       67       56       67      654      456
 7  Friday      238      179      678      345      789      459
 8          ----------------------------------------------------------------
 9              794      563     1090      728     1689     2703
10
11
12
13
14
15
16
17
18
19
20
03-May-88  10:23 AM
```

Fig 7.17 *Result of formatting request - note the stars indicating that the columns are too narrow*

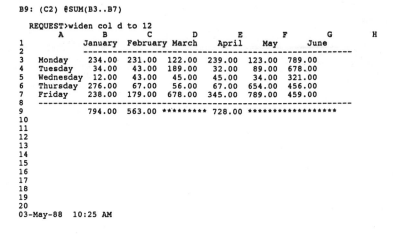

```
B9: (C2) @SUM(B3..B7)

    REQUEST>widen col d to 12
        A        B        C        D        E        F        G            H
  1          January February March    April    May      June
  2   -------------------------------------------------------------
  3  Monday    234.00   231.00   122.00   239.00   123.00   789.00
  4  Tuesday    34.00    43.00   189.00    32.00    89.00   678.00
  5  Wednesday  12.00    43.00    45.00    45.00    34.00   321.00
  6  Thursday  276.00    67.00    56.00    67.00   654.00   456.00
  7  Friday    238.00   179.00   678.00   345.00   789.00   459.00
  8   -------------------------------------------------------------
  9            794.00   563.00 ********* 728.00 ******************
 10
 11
 12
 13
 14
 15
 16
 17
 18
 19
 20
 03-May-88  10:25 AM
```

Fig 7.18 *Remaining two columns to be widened*

```
B9: (C2) @SUM(B3..B7)

    REQUEST>widen cols f to g to 12
        A        B        C            D        E        F        G
  1          January February March        April    May      June
  2   -------------------------------------------------------------
  3  Monday    234.00   231.00       122.00   239.00   123.00   789.00
  4  Tuesday    34.00    43.00       189.00    32.00    89.00   678.00
  5  Wednesday  12.00    43.00        45.00    45.00    34.00   321.00
  6  Thursday  276.00    67.00        56.00    67.00   654.00   456.00
  7  Friday    238.00   179.00       678.00   345.00   789.00   459.00
  8   -------------------------------------------------------------
  9            794.00   563.00     1,090.00   728.00 ******************
 10
 11
 12
 13
 14
 15
 16
 17
 18
 19
 20
 03-May-88  10:26 AM
```

144

Fig 7.19 *Final completed spreadsheet*

```
B9: (C2) @SUM(B3..B7)
   REQUEST>
       A         B        C        D        E        F        G
1              January  February March            April    May      June
2          ----------------------------------------------------------------
3  Monday     234.00   231.00   122.00   239.00   123.00   789.00
4  Tuesday     34.00    43.00   189.00    32.00    89.00   678.00
5  Wednesday   12.00    43.00    45.00    45.00    34.00   321.00
6  Thursday   276.00    67.00    56.00    67.00   654.00   456.00
7  Friday     238.00   179.00   678.00   345.00   789.00   459.00
8          ----------------------------------------------------------------
9              794.00   563.00 1,090.00   728.00 1,689.00 2,703.00
10
11
12
13
14
15
16
17
18
19
20
03-May-88  10:26 AM
```

There are many more spreadsheet "add-ons" available, largely for Lotus 1-2-3, that will perform other useful tasks. For example you can get one that will enable you to plot graphs in three dimensions, another will add to the range of functions already available and specialised packages written to satisfy your particular requirements. Lotus Development Corporation have developed their own word processor that will incorporate Lotus spreadsheets and graphs directly into documents in order to produce reports with text and data displayed in various ways.

TEN POPULAR SPREADSHEET PACKAGES

8.1 VISICALC

Startup command: **VC** or **VCALC**   Command key: /

Command list

B	Blank cell
C	Clear spreadsheet
D	Delete row/column
E	Edit contents of cell
F	Format cells
G	Global (column width, order of recalculation, auto or manual recalc, format)
I	Insert row/column
M	Move row/column
P	Print spreadsheet contents
R	Replicate cell contents
S	Store spreadsheet on disk, load from disk, delete from disk, define default drive, quit Visicalc
T	Title
V	Display Version number of program
W	Window
-	Repeat - character across sheet

The Entry Contents Line, Prompt Line and Edit Line are displayed at the top of the screen. The current cell reference is displayed in the Entry Contents Line together with its contents, if there are any. As an entry is keyed in it appears on the Edit Line and is transferred to the Entry Contents Line when the **Return** key is pressed.

The spreadsheet size is 63 columns by 254 rows. The rows being numbers 1 to 254 and the columns being lettered from A to Z, AA to AZ and BA to BK. Movement around the sheet is performed by use of the arrow keys. The **Home** key takes you to cell A1. Pressing the **>** key brings up the **GO TO:** prompt to enable you to move quickly about the screen. VisiCalc entries are known as **LABELS** and **VALUES**, identified from the first character entered. Labels start with the " character or a letter of the alphabet. Values start with a digit or one of the characters **+ - (. @.**

Functions available

@SUM	Sums contents of cells
@AVERAGE	Averages contents of cells
@COUNT	Counts number of non-zero entries in a range
@MAX	Largest number in cell range
@MIN	Smallest number in cell range
@ABS	Absolute value of a cell entry
@INT	Integer (whole number) part of a number
@SQRT	Square root of a number
@EXP	The exponential (e) raised to power of the number
@MOD	Remainder after division
@LOG10	Logarithm to base 10
@LN	Natural logarithm
@SIN	Sine of angle in radians
@COS	Cosine of angle in radians
@TAN	Tangent of angle in radians
@ASIN	Arc sine function
@ACOS	Arc cosine function
@ATAN	Arc tangent function
@PI	3.1415926536 . . . . .
@NA	Displays **Not Available** in cell
@ISNA	Returns **True** if cell contains @NA
@ERROR	Displays **ERROR** in cell
@ISERROR	Displays **TRUE** if cell contains @ERROR
@NPV	Net present value of a cashflow
@LOOKUP	Looks up value in table

@CHOOSE	Chooses the entry in a cell depending on the numerical value in a specified cell
@IF	Determines the cell to be displayed depending on the result of a test being true or false
@FALSE	Displays FALSE in cell
@AND	Logical AND
@OR	Logical OR
@NOT	Logical NOT

VisiCalc arithmetic is evaluated from left to right and does not follow the normal rules of precedence. You can only export VisiCalc files in DIF (Data Interchange Format). Spreadsheets are stored with a .VC extension.

VisiCalc was originally written for the Apple microcomputer and was also available on the early Commodore series of machines. Later it was adapted to run on IBM PC machines. The program is supplied on one floppy disk.

8.2 SUPERCALC

SuperCalc - Version 1

Startup command: SC   Command key: /

<u>Command list</u>

B	Blank cell
C	Copy cells or cells into another range (cannot make multiple copies)
D	Delete row/column/file
E	Edit contents of cell
F	Format cells
G	Global (column width, order of recalculation, auto or manual recalc, format, border on/off, formula display, cursor movement after entry)
I	Insert row/column
L	Load a previously saved spreadsheet
M	Move row/column
O	Output spreadsheet contents to disk file or printer

P	Protect cells from entry or editing
Q	Quit SuperCalc
R	Replicate cell contents - similar to Copy, but allows multiple copying
S	Save spreadsheet on to disk
T	Title
U	Unprotect cells previously protected
W	Window
X	Execute macro stored in a .XQT file
Z	Zap (erase all contents) spreadsheet

The spreadsheet size is 63 columns by 254 rows. The rows being numbers 1 to 254 and the columns being lettered from A to Z, AA to AZ and BA to BK.

Movement around the sheet is performed by use of the arrow keys. The **Home** key takes you to cell A1. Pressing the = key brings up the **Enter cell to jump to:** prompt to enable you to move quickly about the screen. SuperCalc entries are known as **FORM** and **TEXT** which are identified from the first character entered. **TEXT** entries can start with the " character or a letter of the alphabet. **FORM** entries start with a digit or one of the characters + - (. unless they contain one of the function names.

Functions available

SUM	Sums contents of cells
AVERAGE	Averages contents of cells
MAX	Largest number in cell range
MIN	Smallest number in cell range
ABS	Absolute value of a cell entry
INT	Integer (whole number) part of a number
SQRT	Square root of a number
EXP	The exponential (e) raised to power of the number
LOG10	Logarithm to base 10
LN	Natural logarithm
SIN	Sine of angle in radians
COS	Cosine of angle in radians
TAN	Tangent of angle in radians
ASIN	Arc sine function
ATAN	Arc tangent function
NA	Displays N/A in cell

ERROR	Displays **ERROR** in cell if SuperCalc cannot evaluate the instruction
PI	3.1415926536 . . . . .
NPV	Net present value of a cashflow
LOOKUP	Looks up value in table
FALSE	Displays **FALSE** in cell
AND	Logical AND
OR	Logical OR
NOT	Logical NOT
IF	Determines the cell to be displayed depending on the result of a test being true or false

SuperCalc files are stored on disk with a .CAL extension. If you Output a sheet to disk you are in effect "printing" it and this is saved with a .PRN extension. Help is obtained by pressing the ? key.

Cell references can be entered by "pointing", by which after pressing the **Esc** key the current cell reference is entered into a formula.

This version of SuperCalc is supplied on one floppy disk.

SuperCalc - Version 2

Startup command: **SC2**   Command key: /

This version provided an update of the original version by the addition of an extra command and a number of additional features.

<u>Command list</u>

A	Arrange (sort rows or columns of the spreadsheet)
B	Blank cell
C	Copy cells or cells into another range (cannot make multiple copies); now allows the option of allowing the adjustment of cell references during copying)
D	Delete row/column/file
E	Edit contents of cell

F	Format cells (allows user-defined formats to be created and used)
G	Global (column width, order of recalculation, auto or manual recalc, format, border on/off, formula display, cursor movement after entry)
I	Insert row/column
L	Load a previously saved spreadsheet; now parts of a previously saved sheet can be loaded allowing consolidation of sheets
M	Move row/column
O	Output spreadsheet contents to disk file or printer
P	Protect cells from entry or editing
Q	Quit SuperCalc - now you can quit to another program
R	Replicate cell contents - similar to Copy, but allows multiple copying
S	Save spreadsheet to disk
T	Title
U	Unprotect cells previously protected
W	Window
X	Execute macro stored in a .XQT file
Z	Zap (erase all contents) spreadsheet

The additional functions available in Version 2 are:

MOD	Displays the remainder when one number is divided by another
ROUND	Rounds the contents of a cell to a specified number of decimal places
ISERROR	Displays TRUE or FALSE if the cell expression produces an error
ISNA	As with ISERROR but used in conjunction with N/A
DATE	Displays a date entered in month, day, year form
TODAY	Displays today's date
DVAL	Displays the date when the argument is an integer in the range 1 to 73049
MONTH	Displays the month number
YEAR	Displays the year
DAY	Displays the day number

WDAY	Displays the day of the week (e.g. Sunday is day 1)
JDATE	Displays the Modified Julian Date value. 1 is 1st March 1900

With SuperCalc 2 comes the **SDI** (Super Data Interchange) program (see p 98). This allows the conversion of files from SuperCalc format to Super Data format and Comma Separated Value format and vice-versa. You can also produce DIF files. This version of SuperCalc is supplied on one floppy disk.

SuperCalc - Version 3.1

Startup command: **SC3**   Command key: /

This version of SuperCalc was produced for sale by Amstrad Consumer Electronics for use with their PC1512 and PC1640 series of computers. The main improvement over Version 2 is that it has two additional commands and five more functions. It also, because it is designed for use with IBM PC compatible machines, makes use of the function keys usually found on the left-hand side of the keyboard. The additional commands enable graphs to be generated on the screen, and printed out on your printer, and also enables you to use a SuperCalc spreadsheet as a simple database.

Additional command list

V	View command, define graph type, data ranges, headings, data labels
/D	Database command; defines data range, criterion range, output range, find and extract data

The function keys work as follows:

F1 Help
F2 Erase line
F9 Plot graph
F10 Display graph on screen

The graph types available are Line, Pie Chart, Bar Chart, Stacked Bar Chart, X-Y Graph, Hi-Lo Graph.

Additional functions

PV	Present value of an investment
PMT	Periodic payment of a loan
FV	Future value of an investment
IRR	Internal rate of return
NPV	Net present value of a series of future cash flows at a fixed rate of interest

SuperCalc 3.1 is supplied on two floppy disks. One is a program disk and the other is a Utility disk containing an updated version of the SDI program. In addition to the other features of SDI it contains a utility to convert VisiCalc files into SuperCalc files.

SuperCalc - Version 3.2

Startup command: SC3   Command key: /

This version designed for use on IBM PC and compatible machines offers three sizes of spreadsheet - called Small, Medium and Large. The small sheet has 63 columns and 254 rows, the medium sized sheet has 127 columns and 2000 rows while the large sheet has 127 columns and 9999 rows. The penalty for having a large sheet is a reduced memory space available and slower recalculation speed. You can therefore "tune" your program to take account of the amount of memory you have available and the size of sheet you require. The additional functions available with this version are:

ISNUM	Checks to see if the cell contains numerical data
ISDATE	Checks to see if the cell contains a date
ISTEXT	Checks to see if the cell contains text
ITER	Iteration counter
RAND	Random number between 0 and 1

The same function keys are available in this version as with Version 2.1. The Global command has more options available including one to Keep any changes you have made to the parameters affecting your spreadsheets. In addition it has the ability to perform iterative processes by controlling the number of recalculations performed on a sheet with circular references. Version 3.2 is supplied on two floppy disks, a program disk and a Utility disk. On the Utility disk is a later version of the SDI program that allows you to convert Lotus 1-2-3 files into SuperCalc format files. In addition this disk contains the SIDEWAYS program that enables you to print very wide spreadsheets at right angles to the usual direction of printing.

SuperCalc - Version 4

Startup command: **SC4**   Command key: /

SuperCalc4 is the latest version of this program and it has undergone a considerable change in this update. It has gone a long way towards performing in a similar way to Lotus 1-2-3. The number of functions have been increased and the command list has been changed and extended. The commands can now be executed by keying in the initial letter or moving a highlight using the arrow keys to the required command and pressing RETURN.

Command list

Arrange	Arrange (sort) rows or columns
Blank	Blank out cell or range of cells
Copy	Copy - replaces Replicate and Copy
Delete	Delete cells and files
Edit	Edit entries
Format	Format ranges of cells with user-defined formats
Global	Global command - affects graphics and defaults
Insert	Inserts rows, columns and blocks
Load	Loads spreadsheet file from disk - allows consolidation of files
Move	Moves rows, columns or blocks of cells
Name	Names ranges of cells

Output	Prints spreadsheet to printer or file, now has large range of options to improve the look of output
Protect	Protects ranges of cells
Quit	Leave SuperCalc - to DOS or to specified program
Save	Saves spreadsheet to disk
Title	Title
Unprotect	Remove protection
View	Defines graph parameters and displays graph on screen
Window	Window
Zap	Clear screen
/Data	Database command, defines data range, criterion range, output range, find and extract data
/Export	Exports SuperCalc sheets in 1-2-3, SuperCalc3, XDIF, DIF or CSV formats
/Import	Imports 1-2-3, XDIF, CSV, Numbers, Text or VisiCalc files into Super-Calc4 format
/Macro	Allows you to create macros by a Learn facility, executes macros

Commands used in earlier versions of SuperCalc (such a Replicate and eXecute) are still usable in the latest version even though they do not appear on the command list

SuperCalc4 uses all ten function keys on the left-hand side of the keyboard:

F1	Help
F2	Edit
F3	Name
F4	Abs
F5	GoTo
F6	Window
F7	Resume
F8	Calc
F9	Plot
F10	View

Additional functions provided by SuperCalc4 are:

STD	Standard deviation
VAR	Variance
DAVG	Data management average
DCOUNT	Data management formula cell count
DMAX	Data management maximum
DMIN	Data management minimum
DSTD	Data management standard deviation
DSUM	Data management total value
DVAR	Data management variance
BEGCOL	Number of left column
BEGROW	Number of top row
CHOOSE	Chooses the entry in a cell depending on the numerical value in a specified cell
COLS	Number of columns
CURCOL	Number of current column
CURROW	Number of current row
ENDCOL	Number of right column
ENDROW	Number of bottom row
HLOOKUP	Looks up number in horizontal table
ATAN2	Arc tangent (four quadrants)
INDEX	Value of cell at offset
LASTCOL	Last column number in spreadsheet
LASTROW	Last row number in spreadsheet
ROWS	Number of rows
THISCOL	Number of column with formula
THISROW	Number of row with formula
VLOOKUP	Looks up number in vertical table
ANRATE	Annuity rate
ANTERM	Annuity terms
BALANCE	Remaining balance
KINT	Interest in period
KPRIN	Principal in period
PAIDINT	Interest to period
CTERM	Periods to reach future value
COMPBAL	Compound balance
RATE	Periodic interest rate
TERM	Periods to achieve future value
DDB	Double declining balance
SLN	Straight line depreciation
SYD	Sum-of-the-years digits
ISBLANK	Tests if cell is blank

SuperCalc4 comes on two $5^1/4$ inch program disks and a utility disk or two $3^1/2$ inch disks. The utility disk contains the SIDEWAYS program. The latest revision of SuperCalc4 (Version 1.1) is capable of being used on a network.

8.3 LOTUS 1-2-3

The current version of this program is Revision 2.01.

Startup command: **LOTUS** takes you to the Entry Screen that enables you to select the Lotus worksheet, the PrintGraph, Install, Translate, View of 1-2-3 or Exit to DOS options.

Startup command: **123** takes you straight into the Lotus worksheet.

Command key: /

The Lotus command line consists of a series of options chosen either by moving the highlight bar from one to the other by pressing arrow keys or by keying in the first character of the option chosen.
  The Lotus Control Panel is displayed at the top of the screen. The top line shows the *current cell address* and its contents, including any formats. The middle line is an *edit line* showing the entry as it is made. The bottom line shows a further list of options, if there are any, or a description of the current command. A *mode indicator* is displayed at the top right-hand corner.
  Lotus 1-2-3 requires a minimum of 256K of RAM in order to work. The sheet consists of 230 columns (lettered A to IV) and 8196 rows giving 1,885,080 cells. The size of a Lotus worksheet is governed by the amount of memory you have available after the program has been loaded.

Command list

Worksheet   Covers all the operations performed on the worksheet as a whole - inserting/deletion of rows and columns, global formats, column widths, titles, windows, erasure of the sheet

Range   Covers the formatting of ranges of cells, erasing ranges of cells, protecting and unprotecting, transposing rows and columns and naming of ranges of cells.

Copy   Copies columns, rows, blocks or single cells

Move   Moves ranges of cells about on the worksheet

File   Loads and saves worksheets, combines worksheets, extracts data from worksheets, lists files and deletes files

Print   Prints a worksheet to printer or to a file on disk

Graph   Defines graph parameters and displays graph on screen

Data   Data management: database function, matrix manipulation, regression calculation, data fill (filling ranges with consecutive numbers), data tables

System   Temporary exit (Shell out) to DOS

Quit   Leave Lotus 1-2-3

All ten function keys are used by Lotus. They are:

F1	Help	F6	Window
F2	Edit	F7	Query
F3	Name	F8	Table
F4	Abs	F9	Calc
F5	GoTo	F10	Graph

The entries into a Lotus worksheet are either VALUES or TEXT. To be treated as a VALUE an entry must start with a digit or the characters . + - $ (. The type of entry depends on the first character keyed in.

Functions available

@SUM	Sum of values in a range
@AVG	The average of values in a range
@MAX	The largest value in a range
@MIN	The smallest value in a range
@ABS	The absolute value of a cell entry
@INT	The integer (whole number) part of a cell entry
@SQRT	The square root of a cell entry
@EXP	The exponential (e) raised to the power of the cell entry
@LOG	Logarithm to the base 10 of a cell entry
@LN	Natural logarithm of a cell entry
@SIN	Sine of angle (in radians)
@COS	Cosine of angle (in radians)
@TAN	Tangent of angle (in radians)
@ASIN	Arc sine function
@ACOS	Arc cosine function
@ATAN	Arc tangent function
@ATAN2	Arc tangent function (4 quadrants)
@NA	Value not available
@ISNA	TRUE if cell contains NA
@ERR	Value ERR
@ISERR	TRUE if cell contains ERR
@PI	3.14159 . . . . . .
@HLOOKUP	Looks up value in horizontal table
@VLOOKUP	Looks up value in vertical table
@CHOOSE	Selects a cell value according to size of argument
@RAND	Random number between 0 and 1
@ROUND	Rounds cell value to specified number of decimal places
@FALSE	Logical value 0
@IF	Conditional branch depending on test
@ISNUMBER	TRUE if cell contains a number

@TRUE	Logical value 1
@CELL	Information about the attribute of top left-hand corner of a range
@CELLPOINTER	Information about the attribute of the current cell
@COLS	Number of columns in the range
@INDEX	Value of the cell at the intersection of a row and column
@ROWS	Number of rows in the range
@CHAR	ASCII code for character
@CODE	ASCII code for first character in string
@EXACT	TRUE if two strings are alike
@FIND	Finds position of first occurrence of one string in another
@LEFT	First *n* characters in a string
@LENGTH	Number of characters in a string
@LOWER	Converts string characters to lower case
@MID	Middle *n* characters in a string
@N	Numeric value of top left-hand cell in range
@PROPER	Converts first character in string to upper case, rest to lower case
@REPEAT	Repeat string
@REPLACE	Replace one set of characters with another
@RIGHT	Last *n* characters in a string
@S	String value of top left-hand corner of range
@STRING	Number converted to a string
@TRIM	String without leading or trailing spaces
@UPPER	Converts characters to upper case
@VALUE	Converts numeric characters into a value
@DATE	Serial date number
@DATEVALUE	Serial number of a date string
@NOW	Serial number of current date and time
@TIME	Serial number of a time
@TIMEVALUE	Serial number of time string
@DAY	Day number from date number
@HOUR	Hour number from time number

@MINUTE	Minute number from time number
@MONTH	Month number from date number
@SECOND	Second number from time number
@YEAR	Year number from date number
@CTERM	Number of periods for an investment to reach a future value
@DDB	Double declining depreciation
@NPV	Present value of series of future cash flows
@FV	Future value of a series of equal payments
@ISSTRING	TRUE if cell contains a string
@IRR	Internal rate of return
@PMT	Amount of a periodic payment to pay off a principal
@PV	Present value of a series of equal payments
@RATE	Periodic interest rate for a sum to reach a future value
@SLN	Straight line depreciation
@SYD	Sum-of-the-years'-digits depreciation
@TERM	Number of payment periods of an investment
@COUNT	Counts number of values in a range
@STD	Standard deviation
@VAR	Variance
@DAVG	Data management average
@DCOUNT	Data management count
@DMAX	Data management maximum
@DMIN	Data management minimum
@DSTD	Data management standard deviation
@DSUM	Data management sum
@DVAR	Data management variance
@@	Contents of cell referenced by cell address
#AND#	Logical AND
#OR#	Logical OR
#NOT#	Logical NOT

Graphs generated by Lotus 1-2-3 can be viewed on the screen provided you are using a computer with a suitable graphics screen. To print a graph you have to set up the graph using the Graphics command options and then save the graph, as a .PIC file. Then you leave the Lotus worksheet and from the Access Screen enter the Print-Graph section of Lotus, which is completely free-standing. Similarly if you want to convert files to or from formats such as dBASE II and dBASE III, Symphony and DIF formats then you have to enter the Translate utility, also from the Access Screen.

Lotus 1-2-3 is supplied on six $5^1/_4$ inch or on three $3^1/_2$ inch disks. These are:

System disk	Copy-protected disk containing the Lotus 1-2-3 program
System disk (backup copy)	Copy of system disk in case original disk fails
Utility disk	Contains the Translate program and setup routines for your printer
Install library disk	Contains special driver programs to customise your system
View of 1-2-3	Demonstration programs
PrintGraph disk	Contains the PrintGraph program

You have to install Lotus 1-2-3 on your system and if you have twin floppy disk drives it will only run with a system disk in drive A. The system disk is copy-protected. If you have a hard disk then you can install Lotus to run directly from it by using a utility called COPYHARD. This results in special codes being written to the system disk preventing it from being used again to copy on to another hard disk. Only when you have used another utility called COPYHARD./U can you release your system disk for further use.

Lotus 1-2-3 Version 2.01 files are stored with a .WK1 extension.

8.4 PERFECT CALC II

Startup command: **PC**　　　　Command key: **Esc**

Perfect Calc II commands are displayed in "pop-up" menus overlaid on the spreadsheet. The sheet consists of 52 columns (lettered a - z and A - Z) and 255 rows. Movement about the sheet is by means of the arrow keys. The > key allows you to go to any cell on the sheet. The position of the cursor is shown in the bottom right-hand corner of the sheet. Entries appear in the lower left of the screen as they are keyed in. An entry is identified according to the first character entered. Text is known as a **LABEL** and everything else is a **FORMULA**. Perfect Calc II files are stored with a .PC extension.

Command list

View	Presents commands to move the cursor
Text marking	Marks area to be deleted, copied, sorted or displayed in a different format
Cut & paste	Presents a set of options to allow you to delete, copy, paste, edit or sort
Appearance	Formats ranges of cells
Repeat	Repeats the last command
Datasheets	Presents a set of options to allow you to create, delete, read, print, list and save sheets, also handles consolidation of sheets
Operation	Handles window commands, naming of cells, blanking sections of the sheet
Exit PC	Returns you to DOS

In Perfect Calc II a formula must commence with a = sign. Numbers that are entered must commence with a digit or . or -. Press the ? key for help.

Functions available

sum	Sum of numbers in a range
count	Number of numeric entries in a range
min	Smallest number in range
max	Largest number in a range
avg	Average of numbers in a range
sqrt	Square root
log	Logarithm to base 10
ln	Natural logarithm
round	Round number to specified number of places
abs	Absolute value of a number

int	Integer (whole number) part of an entry
integ	Integration over a range
stdev	Standard deviation
lookup	Look up value in a table
if	Conditional branching
dotpr	Sum of products
slope	Slope of linear regression line
intcp	Intercept of linear regression line
sin	Sine
cos	Cosine
tan	Tangent
rad	Converts degrees to radians
deg	Converts radians to degrees
asin	Arc sine
acos	Arc cosine
atan	Arc tangent
pi	3.14159. . . . . .
not	Logical NOT
and	Logical AND
or	Logical OR
npv	Net present value of series of future cash flows

Perfect Calc II is supplied on two disks. One is the program disk and the other is an installation disk that also contains a series of lessons to help you become familiar with the program. Perfect Calc II is part of an integrated suite of programs consisting of Perfect Writer, Perfect Speller and Perfect Filer as well as Perfect Calc.

8.5 MULTIPLAN

Startup Command: **MP**   Command key: None - the command line is always displayed

The commands are listed across the bottom of the screen and are selected by pressing the first letter of the command. Alternatively you can move through the options by pressing the space bar and selecting the option you want by pressing the RETURN key. The bottom line of the screen is the Status Line telling you the current cell reference, how much of the sheet is free (as a per-

164

centage) and the name of the current sheet (known as TEMP if it is a new sheet). The version of Multiplan described here is Version 3 for IBM and compatible computers.

<u>Command list</u>

Alpha	Places text in the current cell
Blank	Blanks a cell or cells
Copy	Copies contents of cell or range of cells
Delete	Deletes cells
Edit	Edit text or formulas
Format	Formats the display of cells
Goto	Moves to specified cell and runs macros
Help	Help command
Insert	Insert new rows or columns
Lock	Protects cells
Move	Moves rows and columns
Name	Names ranges of cells
Options	Controls recalculation, iteration and sets the audible alarm
Print	Prints sheet on to printer or disk
Quit	Leave Multiplan
Run	Runs a DOS command, audits the relationships between formulas and cells and reports on worksheet information
Sort	Sorts columns or rows
Transfer	Loads and saves worksheets on disk and imports data from an ASCII file
Value	Places numbers or formula in cell
Window	Sets up windows
Xternal	Links with sheets stored on disk

The Multiplan spreadsheet consists of 255 columns (numbered 1 to 255) and 4095 rows (numbered 1 to 4095). Cell references, unlike other spreadsheets, are given in the form **R5C78** for Row 5 Column 78. Movement between cells is made by use of the arrow keys. Information is entered onto the sheet in the form of text (**ALPHA** entry) or numbers/formulas (**VALUE** entry). **VALUE**s must start with a digit or one of the characters =, +, -, . or (.

Functions available

DATE	Serial number of date
DATEVALUE	Date in text converted to serial number
DAY	Serial number to day of month
HOUR	Serial number to hour of day
MINUTE	Serial number to minute of the hour
MONTH	Serial number to month of year
NOW	Serial number of current date
SECOND	Serial number to second
TIME	Serial number of time
TIMEVALUE	Time in text to serial number
WEEKDAY	Serial number to day of week
YEAR	Serial number to year
FV	Future value of investment
IRR	Internal rate of return
MIRR	Modified internal rate of return
NPER	Number of payments of investment
NPV	Net present value
PMT	Periodic payment of investment
PV	Present value of investment
RATE	Rate returned on investment
AND	Logical AND
FALSE	Logical value FALSE
IF	Conditional branch
ISBLANK	TRUE if cell is blank
ISNA	TRUE if cell contains #N/A
ISNUMBER	TRUE if cell contains a number
ISREF	TRUE if cell is a reference
ISSTRING	TRUE if cell contains a string
NOT	Logical NOT
OR	Logical OR
TRUE	Logical value TRUE
ABS	Absolute value
EXP	Exponential (e) raised to power
INT	Integer (whole number) value
LN	Natural logarithm
LOG10	Logarithm to base 10

MOD	Remainder after division
PI( )	3.14159. . . . . .
RAND()	Random number between 0 and 1
ROUND	Round to specified number of decimals
SIGN	Sign of a number
SQRT	Square root
COLUMN()	Column number of cell
DELTA()	Maximum absolute value of changes in value between successive iterations
INDEX	Contents of cell specified row and column
ITERCNT()	Iteration count
LOOKUP	Lookup value in table
N	Value in cell in top left-hand corner of a range
NA()	Not available
ROW()	Row number of cell
S	Text in cell in top left-hand corner of a range
AVERAGE	Average of a list
COUNT	Number of number in a list
MAX	Largest number in a list
MIN	Smallest number in a list
STDEV	Standard deviation
SUM	Total of numbers in a list
CHAR	Character represented by ASCII code
CODE	ASCII code for first character in text
DOLLAR	Rounds a number to specified number of decimals and converts to text
FIXED	Rounds a number and converts to text
LEFT	Displays first n characters in text
LEN	Number of characters in text
LOWER	Converts upper case characters to lower case
MID	Displays middle n characters in text
NAME()	Displays the drive, directory and name of sheet
PROPER	Puts first letter of text in capitals and rest in lower case
REPT	Repeats text n times
RIGHT	Displays last n characters of text
TRIM	Removes leading and trailing spaces from text
UPPER	Converts lower case characters to upper case

VALUE	Converts text consisting of digits to a number
ATAN	Arc tangent
COS	Cosine
SIN	Sine
TAN	Tangent

Multiplan is supplied on three $5^1/_4$ inch disks or on two $3^1/_2$ inch disks and requires a computer with at least 256K of RAM. It is capable of running on a network. You can create and run macros in Multiplan.

8.6 BOEING CALC

Boeing Calc is a spreadsheet that has two very significant differences from all the other spreadsheets mentioned in this book. One is that it has spreadsheets that can exist in three dimensions. This means that a cell reference is to *row*, *column* and *page*. This leads to very large spreadsheets being available so that part of a sheet can be stored on disk while another part is in memory. When a section not in memory is required then part of the sheet is transferred to disk and the required section read into RAM.

Startup command: **BCALC**   Command key: / or **F3**

Command list

Workpad	Covers all the operations performed on the worksheet
Range	Covers the formatting of cells, erasure of cells, protection of cells, transposition of rows and columns and naming of cells
Copy	Copies rows, columns and blocks
Move	Moves rows columns and blocks
Data	Transfers and manipulates data with the sheet, contains the sorting routines
File	Loads and saves sheets, deletes files and allocates a password
Print	Prints sheet to printer or disk

Environment	Determines global parameters, default disk drive, date, time and currency formats
System	Takes you into DOS
Quit	Exit from Boeing Calc

The spreadsheets created by Boeing Calc can be up to 32 megabytes in size. Any sheet can have up to 16,000 rows, 16,000 columns and 16,000 pages. A cell reference has the form of, for example, 10BBG1234 for the cell on page 10 in column BBG and row 1234.

All ten function keys are used by Boeing Calc they are:

F1	Help	**F6**	Window
F2	Edit	**F7**	Input
F3	Menu	**F8**	End keep
F4	Page	**F9**	Calc
F5	Goto	**F10**	Point

Functions available

SUM	Sum of values in a range
AVG	Average of values in a range
MAX	Largest in range
MIN	Smallest in range
ABS	The absolute value of an entry
INT	Integer (whole number) part of entry
SQRT	Square root
EXP	The exponential (e) raised to power
LOG	Logarithm to base 10
LN	Natural logarithm
SIN	Sine
COS	Cosine
TAN	Tangent
ASIN	Arc sine
ACOS	Arc cosine
@ATAN	Arc tangent
ATAN2	Arc tangent (4 quadrants)
NA	Value not available
ISNA	TRUE if cell contains NA
ERR	Value ERR
ISERR	TRUE if cell contains ERR
PI	3.14159. . . . . .

NPV	Net present value
HLOOKUP	Looks up value in horizontal table
VLOOKUP	Looks up value in vertical table
CHOOSE	Selects a cell according to size of argument
RAND	Random number between 0 and 1
ROUND	Rounds to specified number of decimal places
FALSE	Logical value 0
IF	Conditional branching
ISNUMBER	TRUE if cell contains a number
ISSTRING	TRUE if cell contains a string
CTERM	Number of periods for an investment to reach a future value
DDB	Double declining depreciation
FV	Future value of a series of equal payments
IRR	Internal rate of return
PRU	Projected value
PV	Present value of a series of equal payments
RATE	Periodic interest rate for a sum to reach a future value
SLN	Straight line depreciation
SYD	Sum-of-the-years'-digits depreciation
DAMT	Depreciation amount
TERM	Number of payment periods of an investment
GRATE	Growth rate
COUNT	Number of values in a range
STD	Standard deviation
VAR	Variance
@@	Contents of cell referenced by cell address
TRUE	Logical value 1
CELL	Attribute of top left-hand corner of a range
CELLPOINTER	Attribute of current cell
COLS	Number of columns in range
ROWS	Number of rows in range
INDEX	Value of cell at intersection of row, column and page
COL	Current column number

ROW	Current row number
PAGE	Current page number
CHAR	ASCII code for character
CODE	ASCII code for first character in string
EXACT	TRUE if two strings are alike
FIND	Finds position of first occurrence of one string in another
LEFT	First n characters in a string
LENGTH	Number of characters in a string
LOWER	Converts string characters to lower case
MID	Middle n characters in a string
N	Numeric value of top left-hand cell in a range
CLEAN	Removes control characters from a string
PROPER	Converts first character of a string to upper case, rest to lower case
REPEAT	Repeat string
REPLACE	Replace one string with another
RIGHT	Last n characters in a string
S	String value of top left-hand corner of a range
STRING	Converts a number into a string of digits
TRIM	String without leading and trailing spaces
UPPER	Converts string characters to lower case
VALUE	Converts a string of digits into a number
DATE	Serial date number
DATEVALUE	Serial number of date string
NOW	Serial number of current date and time
TIME	Serial number of a time
TIMEVALUE	Serial number of a time string
DAY	Day number from date number
HOUR	Hour number from time number
MINUTE	Minute number from time number
MONTH	Month number from date number
SECOND	Second number from time number
YEAR	Year number from date number

TODAY	Serial number of current date and time (same as NOW)
#AND#	Logical AND
#OR#	Logical OR
#NOT#	Logical NOT

Boeing Calc requires a minimum of 384K bytes of RAM to run and a computer system with hard disk storage. Although Boeing Calc does not have graphics capabilities the associated Boeing Graph program will display data from a Boeing Calc sheet in two or three dimensions. Boeing Calc spreadsheets have a .PAD extension. Boeing Calc has the capability of being used on a network system when the computers require a minimum RAM of 512K bytes and a hard disk.

8.7 QUATTRO

Startup command: **Q**   Command key: /

Quattro commands appear in "pop-up" menus so that selections can be made by moving a highlight bar or by keying in the first letter of the selected option.

Command list

Block	Copy, move, erase and modify the appearance of the spreadsheet
Column	Insert and delete columns, change their width
Row	Insert and delete rows
Erase	Clears all the data from your spreadsheet
File	Retrieve and save spreadsheets, combines spreadsheets, deletes files from disk
Graph	Create, view and print graphs
Macro	Create and run macros
Print	Print your spreadsheet
Layout	Specify windows and titles, alter the way the screen displays the sheet

Default	Change the default settings - hardware used, colours used, display of time, date and currency according to International convention, protects cells, recalculation
Advanced	Sorting, using the sheet as a database, matrix manipulation, regression analysis
Quit	Leave Quattro for DOS

The Quattro spreadsheet consists of 256 columns (A to IV) and 8192 rows. Movement through the sheet is by use of the arrow keys. Across the top of the screen is the Input Line where explanations of the menus are displayed. This line is also used to display the data you are entering into a cell and a prompt when you are expected to obey a system command. At the bottom of the sheet is the Status Line giving you details of the what special keys you may have pressed (the **Caps Lock** or **Num Lock** for example). The date and time are shown in the bottom left-hand corner of the screen and a mode indicator in the bottom right-hand corner. Just above the date and time is the Descriptor Line giving you the Current contents and the format of the current cell. Quattro recognises four types of entry. These are **Numbers**, **Text**, **Dates** and **Formulas**.

<u>Functions available</u>

@SUM	Sum of values in a range
@AVG	The average of values in a range
@MAX	The largest value in a range
@MIN	The smallest value in a range
@ABS	The absolute value of a cell entry
@INT	The integer (whole number) part of a cell entry
@SQRT	The square root of a cell entry
@EXP	The exponential (e) raised to the power of the cell entry
@LOG	Logarithm to the base 10 of a cell entry
@LN	Natural logarithm of a cell entry

@SIN	Sine of angle (in radians)
@COS	Cosine of angle (in radians)
@TAN	Tangent of angle (in radians)
@ASIN	Arc sine function
@ACOS	Arc cosine function
@ATAN	Arc tangent function
@ATAN2	Arc tangent function (4 quadrants)
@RADIANS	Converts degrees to radians
@DEGREES	Converts radians to degrees
@NA	Value not available
@ISNA	TRUE if cell contains NA
@ERR	Value ERR
@ISERR	TRUE if cell contains ERR
@PI	3.14159 . . . . . .
@NPV	Present value of series of future cash flows
@HLOOKUP	Looks up value in horizontal table
@VLOOKUP	Looks up value in vertical table
@CHOOSE	Selects a cell value according to size of argument
@RAND	Random number between 0 and 1
@ROUND	Rounds cell value to specified number of decimal places
@FALSE	Logical value 0
@FILEEXISTS	Detects whether a named file exists
@IF	Conditional branch depending on test
@ISNUMBER	TRUE if cell contains a number
@TRUE	Logical value 1
@CELL	Information about the attribute of top left-hand corner of a range
@CELLPOINTER	Information about the attribute of the current cell
@COLS	Number of columns in the range
@CELLINDEX	The attribute of a cell in the offset position of a block
@CURVALUE	Current value of a menu command
@MEMAVAIL	Amount of memory available
@MEMEMSAVAIL	Amount of expanded memory available
@INDEX	Value of the cell at the intersection of a row and column
@ROWS	Number of rows in the range
@CHAR	ASCII code for character
@CODE	ASCII code for first character in string

@EXACT	TRUE if two strings are alike
@FIND	Finds position of first occurrence of one string in another
@LEFT	First *n* characters in a string
@LENGTH	Number of characters in a string
@LOWER	Converts string characters to lower case
@MID	Middle *n* characters in a string
@CLEAN	Strips control characters from a string
@NUMTOHEX	Hexadecimal value of a number
@HEXTONUM	Numerical value of a hexadecimal string
@N	Numeric value of top left-hand cell in range
@PROPER	Converts first character in string to upper case, rest to lower case
@REPEAT	Repeat string
@REPLACE	Replace one set of characters with another
@RIGHT	Last *n* characters in a string
@S	String value of top left-hand corner of range
@STRING	Number converted to a string
@TRIM	String without leading or trailing spaces
@UPPER	Converts characters to upper case
@VALUE	Converts numeric characters into a value
@DATE	Serial date number
@DATEVALUE	Serial number of a date string
@NOW	Serial number of current date and time
@TIME	Serial number of a time
@TIMEVALUE	Serial number of time string
@DAY	Day number from date number
@HOUR	Hour number from time number
@MINUTE	Minute number from time number
@MONTH	Month number from date number
@SECOND	Second number from time number
@YEAR	Year number from date number
@CTERM	Number of periods for an investment to reach a future value
@DDB	Double declining depreciation

@FV	Future value of a series of equal payments
@ISSTRING	TRUE if cell contains a string
@IRR	Internal rate of return
@PMT	Amount of a periodic payment to pay off a principal
@PV	Present value of a series of equal payments
@RATE	Periodic interest rate for a sum to reach a future value
@SLN	Straight line depreciation
@SYD	Sum-of-the-years'-digits depreciation
@TERM	Number of payment periods of an investment
@COUNT	Counts number of values in a range
@STD	Standard deviation
@VAR	Variance
@DAVG	Data management average
@DCOUNT	Data management count
@DMAX	Data management maximum
@DMIN	Data management minimum
@DSTD	Data management standard deviation
@DSUM	Data management sum
@DVAR	Data management variance
@@	Contents of cell referenced by cell address
#AND#	Logical AND
#OR#	Logical OR
#NOT#	Logical NOT

All ten function keys are used by Quattro, some having several purposes depending on whether the function keys are pressed in conjunction with the **Alt** key or the **Shift** key.

Function key	Unshifted	With Shift	With Alt
F1	Help		Previous Help
F2	Edit		
F3	Names	Macros	Functions
F4	Abs		
F5	GoTo		
F6	Window		

F7	Query	Add-in	What-if
F8	Macro	Debug	Record
F9	Calc		
F10	Graph		

Quattro is almost completely compatible with Lotus 1-2-3 and will read files created by that program without having to go through any translation routine. The graphing facilities offered by Quattro are more comprehensive than those offered by Lotus and in particular a graph can be plotted straight from the screen without having to exit and go to the special graph printing program (PrintGraph) that Lotus forces you to do. If you wish, you can create .PIC files for processing by PrintGraph. Quattro files are stored with a WKQ extension although this can be changed if you wish. Quattro is extremely flexible and you can change the menu structure if you wish and create new menus by using the programs supplied on the **Add-Ins** disk. The program requires 512k bytes of memory to run and is supplied on four $5^{1}/_{4}$ inch floppy disks. These are:

> System Disk
> Resource Disk
> Help Disk
> Add-Ins disk

8.8 LOGISTIX

The Logistix spreadsheet program offers a number of features not available on others. It contains a feature that enables you to produce critical path charts and an enhanced graphics capability that lets you plot up to four graphs on one sheet of paper. Among the graph types available with Logistix is the Gantt chart.

Startup command: **LGX**   Command key: /

Command list

A	Auto - creates and run autos (keystroke macros)
B	Blank - deletes contents of one or more cells

C	Calendar - defines a calendar with times
D	Delete - deletes rows/columns
E	Edit - edits contents of a cell
F	Format - defines formats for one or more cells
G	Global - hides or displays graphics commands, defines relative and absolute cell references, protect cells
H	Heading - selects and fixes vertical or horizontal titles
I	Insert - inserts new rows/columns
J	Join - links data between worksheets
K	Kritical - displays a critical path
L	Load - loads sheet in Logistix, Lotus, SuperCalc, dBASE, text, CSV and DIF format
M	Move - moves row or column
N	Name - names cell or block of cells
O	Output - outputs sheet to file or printer
P	Protect - protects or removes protection
Q	Quit - leave Logistix
R	Replicate - copies one or more cells
S	Save - saves current sheet in one of several formats
T	Table - uses spreadsheet as a database
U	Utilities - performs some DOS operations and displays memory usage
V	View - displays and prints graphs and sets graph parameters
W	Window - window
X	Xecute - enters and executes macros and autos
Z	Zap - clears worksheet

The Logistix spreadsheet has a range of columns lettered from A to AMJ with 2028 rows. Beneath the sheet on the screen is the Status Line telling you the time, the amount of memory used, the reference of the current cell and its type together with its contents. Beneath this line is the Prompt Line and the Help Line with the Entry Line, where the current entry appears, at the bottom of the screen. Entries are **Expressions**, starting with one

178

of the @, +, -, (or . characters, **Text**, which starts with a letter of the alphabet or the " symbol, or **Time** entries which begin with the > character. The case of a cell reference is significant since if you wish to use absolute references the cell reference must be in lower case. Logistix uses six of the function keys on your keyboard. They are:

F1	Help
F2	Files
F3	Recalc
F4	View
F9	Page left
F10	Page right

Functions available

SUM	Sum of values in a range
AVG	The average of values in a range
MAX	The largest value in a range
MIN	The smallest value in a range
ABS	The absolute value of a cell entry
INT	The integer (whole number) part of a cell entry
SQRT	The square root of a cell entry
EXP	The exponential (e) raised to the power of the cell entry
LOG	Logarithm to the base 10 of a cell entry
LN	Natural logarithm of a cell entry
SIN	Sine of angle (in radians)
COS	Cosine of angle (in radians)
TAN	Tangent of angle (in radians)
ASIN	Arc sine function
ACOS	Arc cosine function
ATAN	Arc tangent function
SINH	Hyperbolic sine
COSH	Hyperbolic cosine
TANH	Hyperbolic tangent
RAD	Converts degrees to radians
DEG	Converts radians to degrees
NA	Value not available
ISNA	TRUE if cell contains NA
ERR	Value ERR

ISERR	TRUE if cell contains ERR
PI	3.14159 . . . . . .
E	2.718281284 . . . .
NPV	Net present value of series of future cash flows
LOOKUP	Looks up value in table
CHOOSE	Selects a cell value according to size of argument
RAND	Random number between 0 and 1
ROUND	Rounds cell value to specified number of decimal places
FALSE	Logical value 0
IF	Conditional branch depending on test
TRUE	Logical value 1
COL	Number of columns containing the expression
NCOL	Column number of specified reference
ROW	Number of row containing the expression
DATE	Number of column containing a specified date
TIME	Number of column containing a specified date and time
DAY	Day number
MONTH	Month
MON	Month
YEAR	Year
FV	Future value of a series of equal payments
IRR	Internal rate of return
PMT	Amount of a periodic payment to pay off a principal
PV	Present value of a series of equal payments
COUNT	Counts number of values in a range
DAVG	Data management average
DCOUNT	Data management count
DMAX	Data management maximum
DMIN	Data management minimum
DSTD	Data management standard deviation
DSUM	Data management sum
AND	Logical AND

OR	Logical OR
NOT	Logical NOT
AFTER	Column after latest end of jobs
START	Column of first job
END	Column of last of occurrence of jobs
FLOAT	Total number of columns of "float" in a job
JNAME	Name of job in cell reference
LENGTH	Number of cells taken up by a named job
NWEEK	Week number of column number
NDAY	Day number of column number
DAY	Day of month
DOM	Day and month of column number
DOMOY	Day, month and year of column number
DOW	Day of column number
JDATE	Date number
JDAY	Day, month and year of date number
MOY	Month and year of column number
TOD	Time of column number
TODAY	Current date
TELTIM	Current time

Logistix is supplied on three $5^1/4$ inch floppy disks, two program disks and an examples disk. Logistix files have a .LGX extension.

8.9 ABILITY PLUS

The Ability Plus program contains not only a spreadsheet but also a database, word processor, graph program and a communications package and each of these can communicate with each other so that, for example, a report written in the word processor can include a spreadsheet and a graph both of which remain active within the report. This means that your spreadsheet information can be updated while in the word processor and the graph linked to that sheet will be modified at the same time.

Startup command: **ABILITY**   Command key: **F2**

When Ability Plus starts up it displays a screen with the program options across the top:

DATABASE SPREADSHEET GRAPH WRITE COMMUNICATE PROGRAMS FILES

The spreadsheet is chosen by moving the highlight bar with the arrow keys to highlight the SPREADSHEET option. The spreadsheet is then displayed. At this point the function keys can perform the following operations

F1	Help
F2	Commands
F3	GoTo
F4	Edit field
F5	Pickup
F6	Put down
F7	Shade
F8	Calc/Draw
F9	Flip
F10	Done

Command list

Spreadsheet	Insert, delete rows/columns, titles, windows
Range	Erase or lock shaded ranges
Copy	Copy shaded ranges
Move	Move shaded ranges
Data	Fill ranges, sort and transpose shaded ranges
Print	Print the sheet
File	Save and load sheets
Quit	Leave spreadsheet for main menu

The spreadsheet consists of 702 columns (A to ZZ) and 9999 rows. They are reached by movement of the arrow keys and by the F3 (**GoTo**) key. Entries onto the sheet are identified as **Labels, Values** and **Formulas**, a formula being prefixed by a + sign. At the bottom of the screen is the Status Line indication the contents of the current cell. This line also acts as an entry line.

182

Below this line various prompts and hints are displayed while above it is shown the name of the current spreadsheet together with its drive and directory.

Functions available

ABS	Absolute value
SUM	Sum of list
TOTAL	Same as SUM
COUNT	Number of values in list
AVERAGE	Average of list
AVG	Same as AVERAGE
INT	Integer (whole number part)
LN	Natural logarithm
LOG	Logarithm to base 10
MAX	Largest in list
MIN	Smallest in list
MOD	Remainder after division
SQRT	Square root
PI( )	3.14159 . . . . . .
EXP	Exponential (e) raised to power
ROUND	Value rounded to specified number of decimal places
FACT	Factorial
PERM	Permutations
COMB	Combinations
SIN	Sine
COS	Cosine
TAN	Tangent
ASIN	Arc sine
ACOS	Arc cosine
ATAN	Arc tangent
ATAN2	Arc tangent (4 quadrants)
RAND	Random number
STD	Standard deviation
VAR	Variance
WAVG	Weighted average
IF	Conditional branch
LOOKUP	Look up value in table
COMPOUND	Compound interest
NPV	Net present value
PMT	Amount of a periodic payment to pay off a principal
PV	Present value

FV	Future value
IRR	Internal rate of return
DATE	Date number
DAY	Day of month from date number
WEEKDAY	Day of week from date number
MONTH	Month number from date number
YEAR	Year number from date number
TODAY()	Today's date number
ISERR	TRUE if cell contains an error
INDEX	Value of cell at intersection of row and column
FIND	Find value in a list

Ability Plus is supplied on three $5^1/_4$ inch disks. It can import and export files in various formats. Ability document files have the extension .XTX, graph files have .XGR and spreadsheet files .XSS.

8.10 EXCEL

Startup command: **EXCEL**   Command key:
                                                          ALT, / or **F10**

Excel is a very complex package and so this description is kept short to give a brief concept of what it can do.

<u>Command list</u>

File	Save, load, link and delete files
Edit	Edit contents of worksheet
Formula	Create and define names for cells and groups of cells
Format	Format cells and groups of cells
Data	Use the worksheet as a database
Options	Protection, set various defaults for printing and recalculation
Macro	Record keystrokes into a macro, run macros
Window	Set up windows, hide and unhide windows
Help	Help in general, tutorial, help for converting Lotus and Multiplan commands into Excel commands

The command list is displayed on a MENU BAR across the top of the screen. To select from the menu you can press the underlined letter in the command name, e.g. File, Format or Data. Each selection from the menu will generally then produce a DIALOG BOX. Alternatively a selection can be made by moving through the menu with the arrow keys or by means of a "mouse". An Excel spreadsheet consists of 256 columns (A to IV) and 16,384 rows. The types of data recognised by Excel are:

Numbers	Entries containing digits, a decimal point and a sign (last two optional)
Text	Letters of the alphabet or anything in " marks
Logical values	TRUE or FALSE
Arrays	A matrix of numbers
Error values	#N/A, #NUM!, #DIV/0! etc
References	A reference to a cell either by row and column coordinates (relative or absolute) or by references to cells from the current cell (for example R[-1]C[2])

Functions available

ABS	Absolute value
EXP	Exponential (e) to power
FACT	Factorial
INT	Round down
LN	Logarithm to base e
LOG	Logarithm to specified base
LOG10	Logarithm to base 10
MOD	Remainder after division
PI( )	3.14159 . . . .
PRODUCT	Product of numbers in list
RAND()	Random number in range 0 to 1
ROUND	Number rounded to specified number of places
SIGN	Sign of a number
SQRT	Square root
TRUNC	Integer (whole number) part
ACOS	Arc cosine
ASIN	Arc sine

ATAN	Arc tangent
ATAN2	Arc tangent (4 quadrants)
COS	Cosine
SIN	Sine
TAN	Tangent
MDETERM	Determinant
MINVERSE	Inverse of matrix
MMULT	Matrix product
TRANSPOSE	Transpose of matrix
AVERAGE	Average of list
COUNT	Number of numbers in list
COUNTA	Number of values
GROWTH	Values on exponential trend
LINEST	Parameters of linear trend
LOGEST	Parameters of exponential trend
MAX	Maximum
MIN	Minimum
STDEV	Standard deviation based on sample
STDEVP	Standard deviation based on population
SUM	Sum of numbers
TREND	Values on linear trend
VAR	Variance based on sample
VARP	Variance of population
DAVERAGE	Database average
DCOUNT	Database count
DCOUNTA	Database count of non-empty cells
DMAX	Database maximum
DMIN	Database minimum
DPRODUCT	Database product
DSTDEV	Database standard deviation of sample
DSTDEVP	Database standard deviation of population
DSUM	Database sum
DVAR	Database variance of sample
DVARP	Database variance of population
DATE	Date number
DATEVALUE	Number of date
DAY	Day of month
HOUR	Hour of day
MINUTE	Minute of hour
MONTH	Month of year
NOW()	Number of current date and time
SECOND	Second of hour
TIME	Time number
TIMEVALUE	Number of time

WEEKDAY	Day of week
YEAR	Year number
DDB	Double declining balance
FV	Future value
IRR	Internal rate of return
MIRR	Modified internal rate of return
NPER	Number of payments
NPV	Net present value
PMT	Periodic payments
PPMT	Payment on principal
PV	Present value
RATE	Rate of return
SLN	Straight line depreciation
SYD	Sum-of-years' digits depreciation
AREAS	Number of areas
CELL	Information on specified cell
COLUMN	Column numbers
COLUMNS	Number of columns
INDIRECT	Contents of cell from its reference
ISBLANK	TRUE if cell is blank
ISERR	TRUE if cell contains an error except #N/A!
ISERROR	TRUE if cell contains any error
ISLOGICAL	TRUE if cell contains a logical value
ISNA	TRUE if cell contains #N/A!
ISNONTEXT	TRUE if cell does not contain text
ISNUMBER	TRUE if cell contains a number
ISREF	TRUE if cell contains a reference
ISTEXT	TRUE if cell contains text
N	String of digits converted to a number
NA()	#N/A!
ROW	Row numbers
ROWS	Number of rows
T	Number converted to string of digits
TYPE	Type of contents of cell
AND	Logical AND
FALSE()	Truth value FALSE
IF	Conditional branching
NOT	Logical NOT
OR	Logical OR
TRUE()	Truth value TRUE
CHOOSE	Select value from a list
HLOOKUP	Look up value in horizontal table
INDEX	Selection by index values

LOOKUP	Look up value in table
MATCH	Index of value selected in table
VLOOKUP	Look up value in vertical table
CHAR	ASCII character of a number
CLEAN	Remove control characters
CODE	ASCII code of first character in text
DOLLAR	Round and display in dollar format
EXACT	Tests two strings of text
FIND	Find string within a string
FIXED	Rounds a number and display as text
LEFT	Extracts n characters from text
LEN	Number of characters in text
LOWER	Convert text to lower case
MID	Extracts middle n characters from text
PROPER	Capitalise first letter of text
REPLACE	Replace a string with another string
REPT	Repeat string n times
RIGHT	Extract last n characters from text
SEARCH	Searches for a string within a string
SUBSTITUTE	Substitutes new string for old string
TEXT	Converts a value to text
TRIM	Removes leading and trailing spaces
UPPER	Converts to upper case
VALUE	Converts text to a number

Excel requires a computer of the IBM AT or Personal System/2 type with 640K bytes of memory and a hard disk with at least 5Mb available. It can run under DOS version 3.0 or higher but it can also run under Windows 2.0 or higher and can be used on a network. Excel is supplied on five $5^1/4$ inch high density disks or seven $3^1/2$ inch disks. Files created in Lotus 1-2-3, dBASE and Multiplan can be read by Excel.

INDEX